JALISCO CONDO LAW
In English
Second Edition

a valuable reference for condominiums in Jalisco

translated by Garry Musgrave

JALISCOCONDOS.ORG
HOW TO RUN A CONDO IN JALISCO

Jalisco Condo Law in English – Second Edition
a valuable reference for condominiums in Jalisco

translated by Garry Musgrave

ISBN 978-0-9813533-4-0

Published by:
JaliscoCondosOrg Publishing
#194 – 2416 Main Street
Vancouver, BC
Canada V5T 3E2

Toll-free fax: 800-685-3847
Email: books@jaliscocondos.org

First published June 2011
Second Edition April 2015

Front cover design by Rusdi Saleh
Translation proofreading by Jennifer Nielsen (Spanish 2 English Translations)
Indexing by Garry Musgrave

Dedication

---

*This book and the "**Jalisco Condo Manual**" are both dedicated to my wife Danielle, for her patience during my seemingly never-ending research and re-writes, and for her duties as proof reader par excellence.*

Garry Musgrave

Table of Contents

To properly administer a condominium, whether as a board member or as the administrator/manager, it's vital that you have an understanding of the condominium legislation applicable to your area.

This is true whether you live in a Canadian province, a U.S. state, or a state in México. Condo legislation varies (sometimes greatly) from province to province, and from state to state.

In México, each state has its own condominium legislation, and they can differ significantly. In Jalisco, the condo law is incorporated directly into the state Civil Code. Other Mexican states have a separate condo law.

Many Mexican states base their condo laws on the condominium legislation of the D.F. (Federal District), but some states have changed the D.F. code to suit their needs, or written their own. Jalisco is one of the states that has made significant changes to the condo legislation used in the Federal District.

It's amazing to me how many foreigners living in condos in Jalisco are completely unaware of the condo laws – including those who administer some condos. Or they believe that they are run in the same way as they are in their country of origin. As a result, there are many condos that are being run incorrectly, and aren't following the state law.

There seem to be many opinions and rumours about some of the legal aspects of running a condo here that, while wrong, have become "common practice".

It's equally remarkable to me that the majority of these foreigners wouldn't dream of ignoring state or provincial legislation if they lived in a condo in the U.S. or Canada.

As foreigners in México, we live in a non-English speaking country with a completely different type of legal system. The laws are written in Spanish. In my experience, the main problem that foreigners face when trying to find out what the law says is the lack of good English translations (some I've seen are almost incomprehensible).

This book is the result of over seven years of tweaking and re-tweaking the translations to make them as accurate as possible. This second edition has further tweaks based on experience and feedback from users of the book. It also has many new laws added, all of which relate directly to the running of a condo.

I've also created a unique format where each Spanish article and paragraph in each law has been lined up side-by-side with its corresponding English translation. This lets you easily verify the translation of any articles that are particularly important to you against the original Spanish text.

If you live in a condo *in the state of Jalisco, you owe it to yourself to understand the condo law, your rights and obligations as an owner, and the duties and responsibilities of those who administer your condo.*

If you're part of a condo administration*, you owe it to your community to make sure you're carrying out your duties properly, that the condominium is being run in compliance with the state law, and that you're protecting the property values of all owners.*

If you live in a fraccionamiento *(fracc), you aren't bound by the condo law. However, the condo law is an excellent resource you can use as a model for your association statutes. As well, this book contains a translation of the portion of the Civil Code regulating associations – this very much applies to fraccs. A few of the other laws translated in this book will also apply to your situation.*

The **Road Map** *feature gives you an overview of every book, title, and chapter in the entire Jalisco Civil Code, along with the range of article numbers for each chapter. This feature lets you easily find the part of the civil code that applies to any issue you may have – whether it involves your condominium, or you personally.*

I hope you'll find this to be a valuable resource, and that you'll use it often.

This reference is a perfect companion to my other book, the **"Jalisco Condo Manual – Second Edition"** *– together they are designed to be a powerful tool for those interested in condominium administration.*

Garry Musgrave

Versions of the Laws Used:

Laws and civil codes are living documents that are being continually changed by legislators. It's important that any printed copy of legislation you're referring to is up-to-date.

The translations in this book are based on the most recent versions of the legislation available at the time of publication. The specific version used for each translation is set out in the introduction to its section of the book.

If you're dealing with a critical issue, make sure there have been no changes to the section of the law or civil code on which you're relying, before taking any action.

Blank Pages:

All sections and chapters always start on an odd-numbered page. Because of this, there may be a blank even-numbered page at the end of the previous section or chapter. This is normal. Nothing is missing from your book!

About JaliscoCondos.org:

JaliscoCondos.org is a publisher committed to giving you the most comprehensive and accurate information available about owning and running a condo in the state of Jalisco. It does this by means of printed books, a blog, and other online resources.

Since the first edition was published in June of 2011, legislation has been amended, and I've discovered more laws that are relevant to condo administration. I've also improved the translation and notes of the existing chapters based on experience, plus feedback and questions from users of the first edition.

Here's a summary of the changes made from the last edition:

Throughout the book:

- all introductory and non-translated text was edited for more clarity and additional detail;

- all translations were edited for more clarity, so that the English flows in a better, more natural way (without affecting the meaning);

- vague pronoun references were further resolved, and all gender-specific pronouns such as *"he," "his,"* or *"her"* were replaced with the singular *"they"* form; this issue doesn't exist in the original Spanish, and legislation, in particular, must always be gender neutral; this is much preferable to clumsy and distracting constructs such as *"he or she," "he/she,"* or *"s/he"*;

- inline notes in the translations were added or expanded to more fully explain concepts or legal terms and processes;

- the order of items in the introduction to each section was changed to put the "**Relevance to a Condominium**" section first; and

- typefaces were changed to make the book easier to read.

Part 1 – Brief Overview of Mexican Law: rewritten for clarity, to add details, and to include tips on researching Mexican laws.

Part 2 – Road Map to the Jalisco Civil Code: the even-numbered pages were flipped to make them easier to read along with the corresponding odd-numbered page.

Part 3 – The Jalisco Condo Law: the introduction was rewritten to explain the difference between a condo regime and an association, as well as the difference between condos established before and after 1995.

Part 4 – Co-Ownership: a fourth possibility for co-ownership of the perimeter wall of a condo was added to the introduction.

***Added a new* Part 5 – Obligations of Neighbours:** this contains rules in the *Jalisco Civil Code* that neighbours living anywhere (inside or outside of a condo) must follow.

Part 7 – The Public Registry of Property (formerly Part 6):

- ***new articles*** from the *Jalisco Code of Civil Procedures* ***were added*** that show how publicly registered documents can be used as evidence in lawsuits (important for suing delinquent owners); and

- ***new articles*** from the state *Public Registry of Property Law* ***were added*** to show how preventative injunctions (*see new Part 14*) are dealt with by the registry.

***Added a new* Part 9 – Legal Signatures & Electronic Transmissions:** this contains the *Jalisco Civil Code* definitions of a legal signature, and articles that allow proxies to be emailed or faxed.

Part 10 – Civil Associations (formerly Part 8): the explanation of condos set up before 1995 was clarified in the introduction.

***Added a new* Part 11 – Limitations on Collecting Debts:** this contains the *Jalisco Civil Code* section that restricts collecting fees from delinquent owners to two years.

***Added a new* Part 12 – Income Tax & IVA:** this contains the 2014 federal laws governing the Income Tax, bank account, and IVA (value added tax) obligations of a condo.

***Added a new* Part 13 – Rules for Public Property Auctions:** this contains the state laws governing the public auction held when a condo has forced the sale of a property under *Jalisco Civil Code Article 1032*.

***Added a new* Part 14 – Preventative Injunctions for Lawsuits:** this contains the state laws governing methods of protecting the condo's interests when forcing the sale of a property under *Jalisco Civil Code Article 1032* by preventing title changes, liens, mortgages, or other encumbrances during the process.

Part 15 – Example of Sanctions (formerly Part 9): contains a section of the Condo Law from the D.F. to give an example of sanctions. **This law was changed since the last edition of the book**, and this new edition ***has been updated*** to reflect these changes.

Disclaimer

I've tried to the best of my ability to make sure the English translation is accurate, readable, and of high quality.

I believe that the essence of the meaning has been captured. I've also had the final document proofread by a professional translator, experienced with Mexican legal documents. However, I cannot be held responsible for any inaccuracies or for the consequences of the use of this translation.

I'm not an official translator for legal purposes, nor can this book be interpreted as an official translation.

*It's important to understand that any critical or legal interpretation can <u>only be made using the law as written in Spanish</u>, and **never** by using **any** English translation – regardless of quality.*

*If you have a critical issue that depends on exact and critical wording, **you must examine the original Spanish**. By giving you both the original laws and my translations in a side-by-side format, it's easy for you to verify the translations.*

PART 1 – Brief Overview of Mexican Law

Structure of Mexican Law

Mexican law has six levels. Each level in this list takes priority over the levels below it – **laws in a lower level cannot contradict or change laws in the levels above it**:

1. **Mexican Constitution**: the *Constitución Política de los Estados Unidos Mexicanos* (Political Constitution of the United Mexican States) is the latest Constitution of México.

   Sets out fundamental social rights of individuals. The first such document in the world to do this.

   It's the third official constitution, and was drafted in 1917 during the Mexican Revolution. It's been amended many times – at the time of writing, most recently in July, 2014.

2. **Federal and International Laws**: both carry equal weight.

   The federal government passes legislation for subjects that fall under the jurisdiction of the Federal Government. These laws apply to all states, as well as to all individuals in the country.

   Recognised international laws carry equal weight to Federal Laws, and are those laws contained in bilateral and multilateral agreements signed by México. Some examples are: **NAFTA**, the **GATT**, various UN and other conventions, and Income Tax treaties signed with other countries (Canada is one example).

3. **State Constitutions**: each Mexican state (except the *Distrito Federal* [Federal District or D.F.]) has its own Constitution. They usually lay out the structure of the state government.

4. **State laws**: Each state government (including the D.F.) passes legislation for subjects that fall under the jurisdiction of the State. These laws apply to all individuals in that state only.

   The *Código Civil del Estado Jalisco* (Civil Code of the State of Jalisco) is one such state law.

5. **Regional laws**: regulate a particular area such as a municipality.

   These also have a hierarchy. Municipal subdivisions such as condos and *fraccs* (short for *fraccionamiento*) have their own by-laws or statutes that are below, and must not contradict, those of the municipality (or any higher law). These by-laws apply only to the individual condo or fracc.

6. **<u>Customs and norms</u>**: these aren't written laws, but are the customs and practices commonly observed by the people.

A Civil Law System

Worldwide, legal systems of countries generally fall into one of three main categories: civil law (the majority), common law, and religious law.

The legal system used in Canada, the U.S., and the UK is a **common law system**. However, México uses a **civil law system**.

The main difference between the two is that in common law countries, case law (published judicial opinions) is of primary importance. However, in civil law countries, codified statutes are interpreted by judges on a case by case basis. Usually without regard to previous decisions on similar matters.

The goal of civil law is to give all citizens a written set of codes (laws) that apply to them, and that judges must follow when making their rulings.

In México, both federal and state jurisdictions have codes. The Federal codes take precedence over the state codes (which generally supplement them). Each of the two levels of government have four major codes (*códigos*):

1. a Civil Code – civil laws;

2. a Code of Civil Procedures – civil law processes;

3. a Criminal Code – criminal laws; and

4. a Code of Criminal Procedures – criminal law processes.

The Civil and Criminal Codes (*códigos*) contain the laws themselves, while the corresponding procedural codes (*códigos de procedimientos*) define the legal structure, processes, and procedures used to administer these laws.

Added to these fundamental codes for both levels of government are: the constitutions, codes dealing with specialised subjects, laws (*leyes*) and statutes (*estatutos*), and decrees (*decretos*) and regulations (*reglamentos*). As a body, these form a complete system of legislation.

In general, laws (*leyes*) and regulations (*reglamentos*) are paired in much the way that the Codes and Procedures are paired. The laws are the raw legislation, while the corresponding regulations describe how to interpret and apply the law, as well as defining the structure and powers of the applicable agency responsible (if any).

For example there's a *Ley Federal de Protección al Consumidor* (Federal Consumer Protection Law) that contains the consumer protection legislation, plus a *Reglamento de la Ley Federal de Protección al Consumidor* (Federal Consumer Protection Law Regulations) that lays out the powers of the *Procuraduría Federal del Consumidor* (Federal Attorney's Office for the Consumer), how consumers make reports, and more.

Tips for Researching a Mexican Law

If you're looking into a federal or state *Código* (Code), whether it be civil, criminal or a specialty code, it's important to also look at any corresponding *Código de Procedimientos* (Code of Procedures). This might contain important information about how the topic you're researching is interpreted, managed, or enforced.

Similarly, when looking at a federal or state *Ley* (Law), it's important to also look at any corresponding *Reglamentos* (Regulations). This might contain important imformation about the interpretation and application of the topic you're researching.

Civil Codes

Many Mexican states have a separate condo law, but Jalisco has embedded the condo law into its Civil Code.

Both the federal government and each state have their own Civil Code.

These Civil Codes regulate civil relations between individuals:

- their legal ability to enjoy their rights;
- laws and regulations about marriage;
- organisation of the family;
- personal and real property; and
- civil contracts.

Civil Codes are divided into five main categories:

1. persons (both individuals and legal entities);
2. goods and property;
3. successions and inheritance;
4. obligations; and
5. contracts.

The Jalisco Civil Code

The *Código Civil del Estado de Jalisco* (Civil Code of the State of Jalisco) now in use, was approved by the State Congress on **February 8, 1995**, officially published on **February 25, 1995**, and came into force on **September 14, 1995**.

It's a living document that has been changed by over 50 decrees of congress since then. It's important to make sure you're looking at the latest version of the law before you use it to make a decision about an issue.

Because of this, I've listed the version of the codes (and other laws) I've used for the translation of each section of my book in the introduction to each section.

Structure of the Civil Code

The Jalisco Civil Code follows the format of many Mexican legal documents, and is divided into *libros* (books), *títulos* (titles), and *capítulos* (chapters).

The chapters contain the text of the laws in the form of numbered *artículos* (articles). At the time of publishing this book, there were over 3,100 articles in the Jalisco Civil Code.

Abogados - Lawyers / Attorneys

The job of an *abogado* (lawyer) is to:

- give legal advice to clients, including explaining the legal impact of any proposed actions;

- prepare and explain legal documents;

- represent one of the parties in a legal dispute;

- take part in all types of judicial and administrative processes, acting for the client to the best of their ability before third-parties or in court, according to instructions from the client;

- offer advice and counsel on all legal matters that don't concern the area of work of a *notario*; and

- get help from other professionals (such as a *notario*) when the client's situation calls for it.

Abogados are licensed by the federal government, and can practice anywhere in México. While there are bar associations in México (*Colegios de Abogados*), membership is entirely voluntary.

Although an *abogado* is an expert on the laws of México, they don't usually have the knowledge or expertise to carry out all legal tasks, so they often specialise in specific areas of law (such as family, criminal, commercial, labour, or civil rights).

To make the most effective use of an *abogado,* it's best to use them as a legal or business advisor in the area of law or business in which they specialise. Your *abogado* can then coordinate with any other parties or professionals needed to finish the task (such as a *notario* or another specialist *abogado*).

To enter law school, an aspiring *abogado* needs a *preparatoria* degree (12 years of formal education). Law school itself is another five years.

On graduating law school, they become a *pasante* (clerk) in a law firm or government agency. Once they have enough practical experience, they can present themselves for an oral law examination.

If successful, they receive the designation of *licenciado en derecho* (Degree in Law) and can use the title "*Lic.*" before their name. Make sure this is the case with any *abogado* you hire.

Only take advice from an *abogado* who's licensed in México. Unlicensed individuals are not allowed to give legal advice, even if they have an "*Lic.*" in front of their name.

To prove that they are licensed, they must be able to produce a *cedula profesional* (registered license to practice law). It must have a license number, a photo, and the *abogado's* signature.

To be sure that your *abogado* is licensed, **ask to see their license**, and have the license number included in any written agreement for services before they start work.

Make sure this license has your *abogado's* name on it, and not someone else's. Foreign attorneys aren't allowed to give legal advice or work in México unless they have a Mexican license (few do).

Abogados have somewhat different goals than their counterparts north of the border. An *abogado's* chief aim is **prevention**. Using advice and careful wording of documents and contracts, an *abogado* tries to avoid conflicts – favouring out of court mediation to litigation.

If it becomes necessary to go to court, you must have an *abogado* to aid or defend you. **You're not allowed to be your own lawyer.**

Every court document or presentation must bear the signature of both an *abogado* and his client, to guarantee the proper exercise of the defendant's right to a defence and due process.

Often, an *abogado* will be given the power by his client to appear before the court on the client's behalf (a power of attorney).

As with their northern counterparts, *abogados* must keep any information given to them by their clients privileged.

An abogado cannot transfer the title of a property, and is not to be used for this.

That said, an *abogado* is sometimes used to guide or act for the buyer in a real estate transaction. For example, a buyer might want an *abogado* to carry out a title search, look over contracts and agreements, supervise their interests at the closing, and give them general legal advice throughout the process. An *abogado* can hold deposit money in trust pending the signing of a *convenio de compraventa* (contract to buy property). If a buyer won't be physically present at the closing, they can have an *abogado* there with a power of attorney acting on their behalf.

When buying a condominium property, the buyer's *abogado* can examine the *escritura constitutiva* (registered document that set up the condo) to make sure that the developer has properly set up the *régimen de condominio* (condo regime).

Only an *abogado* will act in your legal interests. A *notario* (more on this later) is neutral, and is not acting for any party. An *abogado* is looking out for the interest of his client.

While it might be tempting to get advice from your personal attorney in your country of origin, unless they're licensed to practice law in México, they can't legally give advice on Mexican legal issues. It's also unlikely they have the specialised knowledge needed. Remember that the legal system in México is significantly different from the U.S. or Canada.

Notarios Públicos - Civil Law Notaries

It's important to understand the difference between a "notary public" in most parts of Canada and the U.S., and a "civil law notary" (*notario público*) in México– despite the similarity in the names.

Civil law notaries have significantly more power, responsibility, and education than a notary public north of the border.

A notary public only has the power to witness signatures, certify copies, take declarations, and administer oaths. A notary public doesn't verify the accuracy of the contents of the document being notarised – the person appearing before the notary public is entirely responsible for the contents of the document.

A *notario* has far greater powers, including the ability to prepare, interpret, and certify all written contracts and legal instruments (such as wills and real estate title transfers).

A *notario* is responsible for the legality of the content of a document, while a notary public only certifies the identity of the signer.

Anyone can become a notary public north of the border. A Mexican *notario* needs much more education and experience.

After first becoming a licensed *abogado* (lawyer), potential *notarios* must then apprentice with an already established *notaría* (notary office) for some time, and must then pass a *notario* exam.

If they're successful, and if a numbered slot is available, they receive an appointment from the state Governor. This allows them to act as a *notario* only in a particular geographical location (typically a town or district).

There are a limited number of *notarios* appointed in any given area (about one per 30,000 population), and no new *notarios* can be appointed until the population has grown to a point where a new position is warranted, or an existing *notario* leaves their practice.

That said, they can work in a *notaría* (notario office) under a licensed *notario* – often the firm where they apprenticed. However, only the licensed *notario* can sign and seal documents.

A *notario* has a great deal more power than an *abogado* (lawyer) because, unlike an *abogado*, a *notario* is conferred with a *fe pública* (public faith) – the power given by the state to attest documents.

A *notario* can use this power to:

- witness the signature of an individual or legal entity (such as a company or association);

- certify the contents of a contract;

- certify the existence of a document (for example, by carrying out a title search); and

- certify official acts or an event that they've personally witnessed.

They can also act as a representative agent for a client, teach, give legal opinions (these opinions are more effective if you get them in writing), and arbitrate between two parties.

Notarios most often carry out their work by issuing an *escritura pública* (publicly registered document) that, once registered, becomes a public record of one or more legal acts such as contracts, agreements, Wills and Testaments, or minutes of corporations or condos.

A *notario* is always used in real estate transactions to transfer title from one party to another through a public document registered at the local *Registro Público* (Public Registry of Property).

Only a *notario* can create and publicly register a document, **an *abogado* cannot do this**.

The *notario's* public power from the state guarantees that these documents have legal validity and certainty. In fact, part of a *notario's* duty of care as a legal expert is to guarantee that all his public documents meet all legal requirements, and that they're in a form that'll make them effective under the law.

A *notario* keeps a copy of every public document that's produced by him, as well as its attachments, in his protocol book (actually a set of bound books). This *protocol* (formal registry) contains the complete set of documents written by the *notario* in chronological order. Each document is numbered sequentially, and forms the official source record of these documents and attachments.

This guarantees that an original copy of the document exists under the care of an impartial third-party who has no interest in the matter.

Once a document has been certified by a *notario*, it can only be nullified or declared false by a court.

The other type of document commonly produced by a *notario* is an *acta* (certificate). This is a certified document where the *notario*, at the request of his client, puts on record under his public faith one or more facts for which he vouches (such as notifications, pleas, or unlawful actions).

The *notario* might only witness the signatures of parties that sign a document in his presence. He can also make a copy of a document, and certify that it's a true copy of the original. In either case, he'll give a *certificación* (certification).

Some of the most common legal tasks carried out by a *notario* are:

1. **Real estate**: when a title of property ownership is transferred, a *notario* must prepare the title transfer document in the form of an *escritura pública* (publicly registered document).

    The *notario* will also get and attach to the *escritura* all required supporting documents such as: a certificate of title and non-encumbrance from the Public Registry of Property, verification of payment of water and land taxes, and an appraisal.

    As well, the *notario* will work out any taxes and fees that are payable to any government agencies involved, and will collect them from the parties.

    The *notario* will then register the new title at the local Public Registry of Property.

2. **Powers of Attorney**: state laws generally require a Power of Attorney to be a public instrument prepared by a *notario* whenever:

    -   the Power of Attorney is of a general nature;

    -   it deals with real estate or real rights;

- an amount of money is declared for the value of the subject of the Power of Attorney that's greater than a set out minimum; and

- the holder of the Power of Attorney is to carry out an act that requires public registration by law.

3. **Wills**: Wills are executed as registered public instruments by a *notario*.

4. **Other documents**: such as minutes of condominium assemblies, minutes of shareholder meetings, incorporation documents, trusts, or mortgages.

Notarios **cannot**:

- act outside of their jurisdiction (usually a municipality or district);

- act against the law or accepted customs;

- act as a legal professional in matters where they're a party to the lawsuit or dispute;

- act as either a principal or an agent for commerce;

- be employees of private companies;

- join or create groups to force others to use their services;

- take political or governmental jobs or appointments;

- act as a minister for a religion or cult;

- serve active military duty; or

- take any other jobs, charges, or duties that are specifically forbidden by the state laws governing *notarios*.

Protocolisation of a Document

The term "protocolise" means to create a permanent record of data or observations on an agreement or proceeding.

In México, it comes from the Spanish verb *protocolizar* (to record or register). It is often inaccurately translated as "to notarise."

There's no one English word for this process as it applies in México, and it's much more complex than the word "notorise" implies.

When a *notario* "protocolises" a document, it means that he will:

- examine it for conformance with applicable laws, and guarantee its enforceability;

- add introductory and closing paragraphs – wrapping the contents into a form that can be legally registered, and that contain the necessary language to make it a certified public document;

- format the content text in an accepted legal form on the special folio paper required by law;

- publicly register it in the local *Registro Público*; and

- add copies of the document, along with any original documents pertinent to it, to the notario's permanent protocol book.

This entire process is what's meant by "protocolisation." Since this word is a far more accurate description than "notorise," I've adopted its use throughout my book.

The Escritura Pública

The form of the *escritura pública* (publicly registered document) is as follows:

- it begins with an introductory section identifying the *notario*, the date, time, and place, the participating parties, and a description of the task for which the *escritura pública* is being prepared;

- next comes a section that contains the actual content of the document such as: an incorporation, the title transfer of real estate, the body of a Will, a Power of Attorney, or the minutes of a condo assembly;

- in the final section, the *notario* will describe the participants and their means of identification, name any parties, documents or laws affecting the *escritura pública*, and certify that the participants were told of the contents and of any impact on them;

- the *notario* will then witness the signatures of the participating parties, and add the certification *"Doy Fe"* (I give faith) – this is the exercise of the public faith given to the notario by the government, and serves to certify the contents of the document.

The *escritura pública* is then registered by the *notario* at the *Registro Público* (Public Registry Office) having jurisdiction. This registration makes the contents of the document binding on third-parties.

The *notario* will keep the original public instrument in his protocol book, and will deliver a *testimonial* (official copy) to both the registry office and the parties involved.

The Escritura Constitutiva

A particular type of *escritura pública* is the *escritura constitutiva*. This is a document that sets up a legal entity (see the next chapter for more info on legal entities).

This document could be the articles of incorporation for a company, the constitution of an association, or the document setting up the *régimen de condominio* (condo regime) for a condominium.

What's a 'Person'?

Constitutions and laws are meant to give rights to (and control the behaviour of) people. As societies became more complex, laws had to regulate more than just individuals.

As a result, modern laws have created structures such as corporations, associations, or societies. These are known as legal persons or **legal entities**, and are treated differently from physical persons or individuals.

Specific laws are generally created to regulate each of these just as if they were a special type of individual. Therefore, a company, an association, or a condo becomes a legal person under the law – with specific laws that apply only to that type of legal person or entity.

This technique lets laws be more easily applied to nonpersons, in a different way than to an individual, and also allows different laws to apply to different types of nonpersons.

For legal purposes, Mexican law recognizes two types of persons:

1. *personas físicas* (people, individuals) and

2. *personas jurídicas* or *personas morales* (legal persons or entities such as companies, associations, or condos).

All persons (both individuals and legal persons) are bound by the rules of law.

Just as in the U.S. and Canada, ignorance of the law is no excuse for violating it. Disuse of a law is also no excuse – if the law is still on the books, it's still enforceable.

Personas Morales or *personas jurídicas* (Legal Entities)

Each state's civil code recognises a number of legal entities. The Jalisco Civil Code recognises about 14 different legal entities that aren't individuals. Refer to *"Part 6 – Legal Entities"* for the complete list. Some examples are:

- federal and municipal governments, and public corporations;

- political parties; labour unions and employers;

- co-ops and mutual benefit societies (including communal farm land such as *ejidos*);

- various forms of Mexican corporations (such as an *S.A. de C.V.*);

- associations, societies, and foundations;

- religious orders;

- **condominiums**; and

- foreigners (this lets the code treat foreigners differently from citizens).

Each of these is a distinct legal entity, and is regulated by a separate and specific section of the Civil Code.

General Laws Governing Legal Entities

Each of the listed legal entities can exercise all rights that don't conflict with their legal purpose, or that aren't forbidden by law – criminal acts, for example. An entity's legal purpose is usually defined either in the law (for example, a condominium), or in its constituting public document (for example, an association).

Further, these legal entities are regulated by:

- corresponding laws (the Civil Code has specific laws for each one, and other laws may also apply);

- their *escritura constitutiva* (the publicly-registered document that set up the entity); and

- their statutes (such as condominium by-laws or association statutes).

The civil code defines the specific rights, obligations, and limits of each legal entity separately.

Since these are entities created by law, and not individuals, they must always have legal and administrative representatives to carry out their rights and obligations.

Since these laws are contained within the Civil Code (and not the Criminal Code), they are to be enforced by any bodies or representatives that act for the legal entity.

For example, in the case of a condominium, this would be the condo's administration. A condo administration has a legal obligation to make sure that the condo is run according to the law.

PART 2 – Road Map to the Jalisco Civil Code

Comprehensive Table of Contents for the Entire Civil Code of the State of Jalisco

In addition to a few other codes and laws, this book mostly contains translations of those portions of the Jalisco Civil Code that I believe are the most relevant to administering a condominium.

However, this barely scratches the surface when it comes to this important piece of state legislation.

The other sections of the Jalisco Civil Code that I've not translated, can also apply to issues that could come up in a condo, as well as in your day-to-day life in Jalisco.

Often you'll be told by people that *"such-and-such is the law,"* or *"you can't do that – it's illegal,"* or, *"of course we can do that – it's perfectly legal!"* Wouldn't it be good to know if they're right? **They're not always**!

This chapter contains a road map that lets you see a summary of **the entire Civil Code at a glance**. Using this Road Map, and the book's index, you can easily find the section of the code that applies to your situation.

While the translation of that section might not be in this book, you'll know where to find the applicable law, and you can have it translated so you can see what it says for yourself. **Knowledge is power**.

The Six Books

The Jalisco Civil Code is divided into six *libros* (books), as follows (**bolded items** in the descriptions have been translated in this book, in whole or in part):

Book 1 – *Disposiciones Preliminares* (Preliminary Provisions)

Book 2 – *De las Personas y de las Instituciones de Familia* (Persons and Family Entities)

> Personal rights of individuals, **signatures**, missing persons, **legal entities**, **associations**, foundations, societies, marriage, common and separate property in a marriage, divorce, provision of necessities to blood relations, paternity and family relationships, adoption, custodial care, childhood, parental authority, guardianship, the Family Council (state or municipal), and family property.

Book 3 – *De los bienes, su propiedad y sus diferentes manifestaciones* (Property, Its Ownership, and Its Different Forms)

Real estate, personal property, abandoned property, possession, usucaption (acquisition of property through long, undisturbed possession), ownership, buried treasure, **co-ownership**, **condominiums**, usufruct (right to enjoy advantages from use of something that belongs to another), rights deriving from use and occupancy, time shares, easements, surface rights, dominion (legal control of property), **rights and obligations of neighbours**, and **the public registry of property**.

Book 4 – *De las obligaciones* (Obligations [**arising from a contract**])

Part 1 – Obligations in General

How obligations arise, **contracts**, the purpose of a contract, the form of a contract, interpretation of contracts, remedies for bad faith or fraud, public liability, instalment payments, rights, subrogation (replacement of the debtor), effects on third parties, compensation, expiration, nullification, revocation, and **termination**.

Part 2 - Untitled [debt and creditors]

Insolvency of creditors, preferred debt, mortgages, pignorative contracts (when a property owner lets someone who has lent him money the right to use and enjoy the property until the debt is paid back), and preferred creditors.

Book 5 – *De las diversas especies de contratos* (The Various Types of Contracts)

The promise to enter into a contract, options, letters of intent, sales contracts, barters and trades, donations, consumption loans (a loan of personal goods intended to be consumed by the borrower, and to be returned to the lender in kind), leases, sub-leasing, commodatum (grant of free and temporary use of a fixed asset), deposits, **powers of attorney**, contracts for services, freight contracts, hotels and guest houses, agricultural partnerships (sharecropping), wagers, life annuities, futures contracts, guaranties (one person assumes responsibility for payment of another's debt), collateral (pledge of security on debt), mortgages, arbitration agreements, and transactions (a civil law term for a contract by which the parties end a current dispute or prevent a future one by making mutual concessions).

Book 6 – *De las sucesiones* (Succession [and Inheritance])

Succession by Will, heirs and inheritances in general, substitutions (different heirs inherit under different circumstances), nullification, revocation, and expiry of a Will, types of Wills, recognition of Wills from other Mexican states, recognition of Wills made in foreign countries (by Mexicans), inheritance rules, and executors and trustees.

Format of the Road Map

The Road Map has three columns, containing:

1. The Spanish names of each of the *libros* (books), *títulos* (titles), and *capítulos* (chapters) in the Jalisco Civil Code. Each of these types of division has been highlighted differently to make them obvious.

2. The English translation of the first column.

3. Notes about important concepts, plus the range of article numbers contained in each *capítulo* (chapter).

   Since many technical legal terms are still incomprehensible to the average person when translated into English, I've included definitions for them in the Notes column (for example, usucaption, subrogation, and caducity).

How to Use the Road Map

There are three ways you can use the Road Map:

1. Use the overview of the six books earlier in this chapter to narrow your search down to a particular book, and then look at the titles belonging to that book in the Road Map. If a particular title seems applicable to your situation, then read the names of the chapters in it.

   I recommend reading through the entire Road Map at least once to give yourself a good overview of the various issues dealt with in the Jalisco Civil Code.

2. The Road Map is also indexed. Look at the "**Road Map**" entry in the index at the back of this book for a list of topics, and the Road Map page where you'll find the corresponding code chapter (along with its title and book).

   Many important topics are also listed separately in the index, and will have a "**Road Map (in the)**" index entry pointing to the Road Map page with the corresponding chapter.

3. If you want to find a section of code by its article number, look in the notes column of the Road Map to find the range of articles containing the one you're looking for. This will tell you the book, title, and chapter of the Jalisco Civil Code that contains that article number.

   Although the civil code is changed a few of times a year, the article numbers don't change. If new articles are added, the original numbering is unchanged. For example, if they put in a new article between articles 2021 and 2022, it will be numbered **2021 bis (2021a)**. If an article is removed, its number is kept, and the article text will be replaced by "*Derogado*" (Repealed).

English	Spanish	Articles / Notes
Book 1 - Preliminary Provisions	**Libro Primero - Disposiciones Preliminares**	No titles or chapters. Articles 1 through 17.
Book 2 - Persons and Family Entities	**Libro Segundo - De las Personas y de las Instituciones de Familia**	
<u>Title 1 - Individuals</u>	<u>Título Primero - De las Personas Físicas</u>	
Chapter I - General Provisions	**Capítulo I** – Disposiciones Generales	**Articles 18 through 23.**
Chapter II - Rights of Legal Capacity	**Capítulo II** – De los Derechos de Personalidad	**Articles 24 through 40.**
Chapter III - Private Information	**Capítulo III** – De la Información Privada	Privacy legislation passed in September 2004. **Articles 40a1 through 40a39.**
Chapter IV - The Estate	**Capítulo IV** – Del Patrimonio	**Articles 41 through 45.**
Chapter V - The Age of Majority	**Capítulo V** – De la Mayoría de Edad	**Articles 46 through 47.**
Chapter IV - The Age of Minority and Incapacity	**Capítulo VI** – De la Minoría de Edad e Incapacidad	**Articles 48 through 49.**
Chapter VII - Interdiction [court ordered guardianship]	**Capítulo VII** – Del Estado de Interdicción	**Articles 50 through 55.**
Chapter VIII - Emancipation	**Capítulo VIII** – De la Emancipación	In civil law, **emancipation** is the termination of parental control. **Articles 56 through 59.**
Chapter IX - Characteristics of the individual	**Capítulo IX** – De la Individualización de las Personas Físicas	Form of a person's name using given names and family names. Signatures. Articles 68 to 71 are translated in *"Part 9 – Legal Signatures & Electronic Transmissions."* **Articles 60 through 71.**
Chapter X - Residence	**Capítulo X** – Del Domicilio	**Articles 72 through 76.**
Chapter XI - Marital Status	**Capítulo XI** – Del Estado Civil	**Articles 77 through 86.**

Título Segundo - De los Ausentes e Ignorados / Title 2 - The Missing and the Unknown

Capítulo I – Disposiciones Generales	Chapter I - General Provisions	Articles 87 through 90.
Capítulo II – De las Medidas Provisionales en caso de Ausencia	Chapter II - Provisional Measures in the Case of a *Missing Person*	Articles 91 through 109.
Capítulo III – De la Declaración de Ausencia	Chapter III - The Declaration of *Being* Missing	Articles 110 through 120.
Capítulo IV – De los Efectos de la Declaración de Ausencia	Chapter IV - Effects of the Declaration of *Being* Missing	Articles 121 through 139.
Capítulo V – De la Administración de los Bienes del Ausente Casado	Chapter V - Administration of the Assets of a Missing Spouse	Articles 140 through 145.
Capítulo VI – De la Presunción de Muerte del Ausente	Chapter VI - Presumption of Death of the *Missing Person*	Articles 146 through 155.
Capítulo VII – De los Efectos de la Ausencia respecto de los Derechos Eventuales del Ausente	Chapter VII - Effects of Absence With Respect to the Eventual Rights of the *Missing Person*	Articles 156 through 160.

Título Tercero - De las Personas Jurídicas / Title 3 - Legal Entities

Capítulo I – Disposiciones Generales	Chapter I - General Provisions	Chapter translated in "*Part 6 – Legal Entities*." **Articles 161 through 171.**
Capítulo II – De las Asociaciones	Chapter II - Associations	Chapter translated in "*Part 10 – Civil Associations*." **Articles 172 through 189.**
Capítulo III – De las Fundaciones	Chapter III - Foundations	**Articles 190 through 207.**
Capítulo IV – De las Sociedades	Chapter IV - Societies	Corporations in México are societies. A common form is the S.A. de C.V. (*Sociedad Anónima de Capital Variable*). **Articles 208 through 219.**
Capítulo V – De los Socios	Chapter V - Partners [in companies]	*Socio* also means members of a society. **Articles 220 through 225.**

Capítulo (Spanish)	Chapter (English)	Articles
Capítulo VI – De la Administración de la Sociedad	Chapter VI - Administration of a Society [or company]	**Articles 226 through 237.**
Capítulo VII – De la Disolución de las Sociedades	Chapter VII - Dissolution of a Society [or company]	**Articles 238 through 243.**
Capítulo VIII – De la Liquidación de la Sociedad	Chapter VIII - Liquidation of a Society [or company]	**Articles 244 through 254.**
Capítulo IX – De las Sociedades Extranjeras	Chapter IX - Foreign Companies	**Articles 255 through 257.**

Título Cuarto - Del Matrimonio / Title 4 - Marriage

Capítulo (Spanish)	Chapter (English)	Articles
Capítulo I – Disposiciones Generales	Chapter I - General Provisions	**Articles 258 through 259.**
Capítulo II – De los Requisitos para Contraer Matrimonio	Chapter II - Requirements to Get Married	**Articles 260 through 272.**
Capítulo III – De los Deberes y Derechos que Nacen del Matrimonio	Chapter III - Obligations and Rights That Arise From Marriage	**Articles 273 through 279.**
Capítulo IV – De las Relaciones Económico-Patrimoniales entre los Cónyuges	Chapter IV - Economic and Property Relationships Between the Spouses	**Articles 280 through 286.**
Capítulo V – De la Sociedad Legal	Chapter V - The Legal Partnership	Refers to the partnership between the spouses, and the combining of property created by the marriage contract. **Articles 287 through 288.**
Capítulo VI – De la Sociedad Conyugal o Voluntaria	Chapter VI - The Conjugal Partnership or Voluntary Partnership	**Articles 289 through 295.**
Capítulo VII – Disposiciones Comunes a las Sociedades Legal y Conyugal	Chapter VII - Provisions Common to Legal and Conjugal Partnerships	Administration and control of common assets, common and separate property, liquidation of assets. **Articles 286 through 349.**
Capítulo VIII – De la Separación de Bienes	Chapter VIII - Division of Assets	**Articles 350 through 357.**

Spanish	English	Articles
Capítulo II – De los Efectos de la Patria Potestad respecto de los Bienes del Hijo	**Chapter II** - Effects of Parental Authority With Respect to the property of the Child	**Articles 588 through 596.**
Capítulo III – De los Modos de Acabarse y suspenderse la Patria Potestad	**Chapter III** - The Ways of Ending and Suspending Parental Authority	**Articles 597 through 602.**
Título Noveno - De la Tutela	**Title 9 - Guardianship**	
Capítulo I – Disposiciones Generales	**Chapter I** - General Provisions	**Articles 603 through 622.**
Capítulo II – De la Tutela Testamentaria	**Chapter II** - Testamentary Guardianship	Appointment of a guardian in a Will. **Articles 623 through 634.**
Capítulo III – De la Tutela Legítima de los Menores	**Chapter III** - Legal Guardianship of Minors	**Articles 635 through 639.**
Capítulo IV – De la Tutela Legítima del Mayor Incapacitado	**Chapter IV** - Legal Guardianship of Incapacitated Seniors	**Articles 640 through 647.**
Capítulo V – De la Tutela Dativa	**Chapter V** - Guardianship by Court Appointment	**Articles 648 through 653a.**
Capítulo VI – De las Personas Inhábiles para el Desempeño de la Tutela y de las que deben ser separadas de ella	**Chapter VI** - People Incapable of Carrying Out Guardianship *Responsibilities* Should Be Removed From *Guardianship*	**Articles 654 through 660.**
Capítulo VII – De las Excusas para el Desempeño de la Tutela	**Chapter VII** - Exemptions From the Performance of Guardianship	**Articles 661 through 668.**
Capítulo VIII – De la Garantía que deben prestar los Tutores para asegurar su manejo	**Chapter VIII** - Guarantee Rendered by Guardians to Make Sure of Their Handling *of the Guardianship*	They must post a bond or collateral. **Articles 669 through 683.**
Capítulo IX – Del Desempeño de la Tutela	**Chapter IX** - Performance of the Guardianship	**Articles 684 through 686.**
Capítulo X – De la Tutela del Menor	**Chapter X** - Guardianship of a Minor	**Articles 687 through 693.**
Capítulo XI – Reglas sobre la administración de bienes	**Chapter XI** - Rules About the Administration of Assets	**Articles 694 through 733.**
Capítulo XII – De las cuentas de la tutela	**Chapter XII** - Guardianship Accounts	**Articles 734 through 749.**
Capítulo XIII – De la extinción de la tutela	**Chapter XIII** - Termination of Guardianship	**Article 750**

Título Tercero - De la posesión	**Title 3 - Possession**	
Capítulo Unico	Only Chapter [a single chapter only] – Untitled	**Articles 840 through 878.**
Título Cuarto - De la usucapión	**Title 4 - Usucaption**	
Capítulo I – Disposiciones generales	**Chapter I** - General Provisions	**Usucaption** is a legal term meaning the acquisition of property through long, undisturbed possession. **Articles 879 through 897.**
Capítulo II – De la titulación por usucapión	**Chapter II** - Awarding Title by Usucaption	**Articles 898 through 899.**
Título Quinto - De la propiedad	**Title 5 - Ownership**	
Capítulo I – Disposiciones generales	**Chapter I** - General Provisions	**Articles 900 through 905.**
Capítulo II – De los tesoros	**Chapter II** - Treasure	Buried or hidden treasure found on a property. **Articles 906 through 916.**
Capítulo III – Del derecho de accesión	**Chapter III** - Right of Accession	**Accession** is the right to own things that become a part of something already owned. A property owner has the right to everything that is produced on, added to, or incorporated into the property – even by others. **Articles 917 through 960.**
Capítulo IV – De la copropiedad	**Chapter IV** - Co-Ownership	Chapter translated in *"Part 4 – Co-Ownership."* **Articles 961 through 1000.**

Título Sexto - Del condominio	Title 6 - The Condominium	Title translated in "*Part 3 – The Jalisco Condo Law.*"
Capítulo I – Prevenciones generales	**Chapter I** - General Provisions	Definitions, setting up the condo regime, by-laws, common property, owner's obligations and rights, maintenance and repairs, and improvements. **Articles 1001 through 1010.**
Capítulo II – De la administración	**Chapter II** - The Administration	Appointment and duties and obligations of the Administrator. **Articles 1011 through 1013a.**
Capítulo III – Del consejo de administración	**Chapter III** - The Administrative Council [**Board**]	Make up, appointment, and duties and obligations of the Council (Board). **Articles 1014 through 1018.**
Capítulo IV – De las asambleas	**Chapter IV** - Assemblies	Supreme authority, ordinary and extraordinary assemblies, assembly call notice, and voting on resolutions. **Articles 1019 through 1025.**
Capítulo V – De las cuotas	**Chapter V** - Fees	Owners must pay, reserve funds, late interest, owner's accounts, and special assessments. **Articles 1026 through 1030.**
Capítulo VI – De las controversias	**Chapter VI** - Disputes	Disputes between owners arbitrated by Council, forced sale of property, and forced eviction of a tenant. **Articles 1031 through 1033.**
Capítulo VII – De la destrucción y extinción	**Chapter VII** - Destruction and Termination	**Article 1034.**
Capítulo VIII – De los condominios habitacionales duplex	**Chapter VII** - Residential Duplexes	**Articles 1035 through 1038.**

Spanish	English	Articles
Título Séptimo - Del usufructo	**Title 7 - Usufruct**	
Capítulo I – Del usufructo en general	**Chapter I** - Usufruct in General	**Usufruct** is a legal term meaning the right to enjoy benefits from the use of something that belongs to another. **Articles 1039 through 1049.**
Capítulo II – De los derechos del usufructuario	**Chapter II** - Rights of the Beneficial Occupant	**Articles 1050 through 1064.**
Capítulo III – De las obligaciones del usufructuario	**Chapter III** - Obligations of the Beneficial Occupant	**Articles 1065 through 1096.**
Capítulo IV – De los modos de extinguirse el usufructo	**Chapter IV** - Ways of Terminating the *Right of* Usufruct	**Articles 1097 through 1106.**
Título Octavo - Del uso y de la habitación	**Title 8 - Use and Occupancy**	
Capítulo Unico	**Only Chapter** [a single chapter only] – Untitled	**Articles 1107 through 1114.**
Título Noveno – Derecho de uso en tiempo compartido	**Title 9 - Right of Use for Time Shares**	
Capítulo I – Disposiciones generales	**Chapter I** - General Provisions	**Articles 1115 through 1121.**
Capítulo II – Derechos y obligaciones	**Chapter II** - Rights and Obligations	**Articles 1122 through 1131.**
Capítulo III – Cuotas de mantenimiento	**Chapter III** - Maintenance Fees	**Articles 1132 through 1133.**
Capítulo IV – Pérdida de derechos	**Chapter IV** - Loss of Rights	**Articles 1134 through 1138.**
Capítulo V – Sanciones	**Chapter V** - Sanctions	**Article 1139.**
Título Decimo - De las servidumbres	**Title 10 - Easements**	
Capítulo I – Disposiciones generales	**Chapter I** - General Provisions	**Articles 1140 through 1147.**
Capítulo II – De las servidumbres legales	**Chapter II** - Easements *Established* by Law	**Articles 1148 through 1150.**
Capítulo III – De la servidumbre legal de desagüe	**Chapter III** - Easements *Established* by Law for Drainage	**Articles 1151 through 1157.**

Spanish	English	Articles
Capítulo IV – De la servidumbre legal de acueductos	Chapter IV - Easements *Established* by Law for Water Lines	Articles 1158 through 1174.
Capítulo V – De la servidumbre legal de paso	Chapter V - Easements *Established* by Law for Passage	Articles 1175 through 1187.
Capítulo VI – De las servidumbres voluntarias	Chapter VI - Easements by Agreement	Articles 1188 through 1191.
Capítulo VII – De cómo se adquieren las servidumbres voluntarias	Chapter VII - How to Acquire Easements by Agreement	Articles 1192 through 1196.
Capítulo VIII – Derechos y obligaciones de los propietarios de los predios entre los que está constituida alguna servidumbre voluntaria	Chapter VIII - Rights and Obligations of the Owners of Properties Between Which Easements by Agreement Are Created	Articles 1197 through 1205.
Capítulo IX – De la extinción de las servidumbres	Chapter IX - Termination of Easements	Articles 1206 through 1212.
Título Decimoprimero - Del derecho de superficie	Title 11 - Surface Rights	
Capítulo Unico	Only Chapter [a single chapter only] – Untitled	Articles 1213 through 1223.
Título Decimosegundo - De las limitaciones de dominio	Title 12 - Limitations of Domain [legal control over property]	
Capítulo Unico	Only Chapter [a single chapter only] – Untitled	Articles 1224 through 1227.
Título Decimotercero - De los derechos y obligaciones de la vecindad	Title 13 - Rights and Obligations of Neighbours	
Capítulo Unico	Only Chapter [a single chapter only] – Untitled	Title translated in "*Part 5 – Obligations of Neighbours.*" Articles 1228 through 1251.

Título Decimocuarto - Del Registro Público de la Propiedad	**Title 14 - The Public Registry of Property**	
Capítulo Único	Only Chapter [a single chapter only] – Untitled	Chapter translated in "*Part 7 – The Public Registry of Property.*" **Articles 1252 through 1258.**
Libro Cuarto - De las obligaciones	**Book 4 - Obligations**	
Libro Cuarto Primera Parte - De las obligaciones en general	**Book 4 Part 1 - Obligations in General**	
Título Primero - Fuentes de las obligaciones	**Title 1 - Sources of Obligations**	
Capítulo I – Disposiciones generales	**Chapter I** - General Provisions	Article 1261 is translated in "*Part 9 – Legal Signatures & Electronic Transmissions.*" **Articles 1259 through 1263.**
Capítulo II – De los contratos	**Chapter II** - Contracts	Validity of, capacity to enter, representation, consent to, subjects and causes, form of, clauses, and interpretation. Article 1308 is translated in "*Part 9 – Legal Signatures & Electronic Transmissions.*" **Articles 1264 through 1329.**
Capítulo III – De la declaración unilateral de la voluntad	**Chapter III** - Declaration of Willingness by One Party	Acceptance of a public offer implies a contract. **Articles 1330 through 1355.**
Capítulo IV – Del enriquecimiento ilegítimo	**Chapter IV** - Illegitimate Enrichment	Remedies for bad faith or fraudulent contracts. **Articles 1356 through 1369.**
Capítulo V – De la gestión de negocios	**Chapter V** - Business Negotiations	**Articles 1370 through 1386.**
Capítulo VI – De las obligaciones que nacen de hechos ilícitos	**Chapter VI** - Obligations Arising From Illegal Activities	**Articles 1387 through 1426.**

Capítulo VII – De la responsabilidad civil objetiva	**Chapter VII** - Public Liability	Liability for damage to others caused by the use of dangerous, high speed, explosive, high current (electrical) or other similar devices or materials. **Articles 1427 through 1431.**
Capítulo VIII – De las ventas por autoridad	**Chapter VIII** - Sales by Public Authorities	Public authorities can force an individual to sell their property at public auction by executive or judicial order **Articles 1432 through 1446.**
Título Segundo – Modalidades de las obligaciones	**Title 2 - Types of Obligations**	
Capítulo I – De las obligaciones condicionales	**Chapter I** - Conditional Obligations	**Articles 1447 through 1457.**
Capítulo II – De las obligaciones a plazo	**Chapter II** - *Payments* by Instalment	**Articles 1458 through 1465.**
Capítulo III – De las obligaciones conjuntivas y alternativas	**Chapter III** - Conjunctive and Alternative Obligations	**Conjunctive obligations** are a group of obligations, all of which must be met. **Alternative obligations** are a group of obligations, any one of which must be met. **Articles 1466 through 1488.**
Capítulo IV – De las obligaciones mancomunadas	**Chapter IV** - Joint Obligations	Obligations involving two or more debtors. **Articles 1489 through 1518.**
Capítulo V – De las obligaciones de dar	**Chapter V** - Obligations to Turn Over	Obligation results in transfer of control over an asset. **Articles 1519 through 1534.**
Capítulo VI – De las obligaciones de hacer o de no hacer	**Chapter VI** - Obligations to Do or Not To Do	Remedies for work not performed according to the contract. **Articles 1535 through 1536.**
Título Tercero - De la transmisión de las obligaciones	**Title 3 - Transfer of Obligations**	
Capítulo I – De la cesión de derechos	**Chapter I** - Assignment of Rights	**Articles 1537 through 1563.**

Capítulo II – De la sustitución de deudor	**Chapter II** - Substitution of the Debtor	**Articles 1564 through 1570.**
Capítulo III – De la subrogación	**Chapter III** - Subrogation	**Subrogation** is a legal term essentially meaning substitution of the creditor. **Articles 1571 through 1576.**
Título Cuarto - Efectos de las obligaciones	**Title 4 - Effects of Obligations**	
Capítulo I – Efectos de las obligaciones entre las partes	**Chapter I** - Effects of Obligations Between Parties	**Articles 1577 through 1665.**
Capítulo II – Efectos de las obligaciones con relación a tercero	**Chapter II** - Effects of Obligations With Respect to a Third Party	**Articles 1666 through 1690.**
Título Quinto - Extinción de las obligaciones	**Title 5 - Termination of Obligations**	
Capítulo I – De la compensación	**Chapter I** - Compensation	**Articles 1691 through 1712.**
Capítulo II – De la confusión de derechos	**Chapter II** - Confusion of Rights	**Confusion of rights** is when a debtor and creditor become the same legal person, there's a confusion of rights which extinguishes the debt. For example, if a woman debtor marries her creditor, the debt is extinguished. **Articles 1713 through 1715.**
Capítulo III – De la remisión de la deuda	**Chapter III** - Forgiving the Debt	**Articles 1716 through 1719.**
Capítulo IV – De la novación	**Chapter IV** - Changing the Obligation	**Articles 1720 through 1731.**
Capítulo V – Prescripción	**Chapter V** - Prescription	**Prescription** is a process where an obligation can be removed by the court because of the long passage of time. Articles 1732 to 1748 are translated in *"Part 11 – Limitations on Collecting Debts."* **Articles 1732 through 1753.**

Spanish	English	Articles / Description
Capítulo VI – La caducidad	**Chapter VI - Caducity**	**Caducity** is the termination of an obligation after a specified period of time, or the non-realisation of specified acts. **Articles 1754 through 1758.**
Título Sexto	**Title 6 - Untitled**	Concerned with various ways contracts can be nullified.
Capítulo I – De la nulidad y de otras formas de ineficacia	**Chapter I - Invalidity and Other Types of Ineffectiveness**	**Articles 1759 through 1779.**
Capítulo II – De la revocación	**Chapter II - Cancellation**	**Articles 1780 through 1782.**
Capítulo III – De la resolución o rescisión	**Chapter III - Resolution or Extinguishment**	**Articles 1783 through 1792.**
Capítulo IV – De la inoponibilidad	**Chapter IV - Inadmissibility**	**Article 1793.**
Capítulo V – De la inoficiocidad	**Chapter V -** *Inoficiocidad* **[no English translation]**	*Inoficiocidad* means anything done contrary to an assumed obligation. **Article 1794.**
Capítulo VI – De la reducibilidad	**Chapter VI -** *Reducibilidad* **[no English translation]**	*Reducibilidad* is when a contract grants one party greater benefits than those established in law. It doesn't terminate the contract, but reestablishes equity by reducing or annulling the benefits in question. **Article 1795.**
Libro Cuarto Segunda Parte	**Book 4 Part 2 - Untitled [debt & creditors]**	
Título Primero - De la concurrencia y graduación de créditos y de la insolvencia de los deudores	**Title 1 - Concurrence and Order of Precedence of Debtors and Insolvency of Debtors**	
Capítulo I – Disposiciones generales	**Chapter I - General Provisions**	**Articles 1796 through 1814.**

Spanish	English	Description / Articles
Capítulo II – De los créditos privilegiados, hipotecarios y pignoraticios	**Chapter II** - Preferred Debts, Mortgages, and Pignorative Contracts	A **pignorative contract** is when a property owner allows someone who has lent him money the right to use and enjoy the property until the debt is paid back. **Articles 1815 through 1827.**
Capítulo III – De los acreedores preferentes sobre determinados bienes	**Chapter III** - Preferred Creditors for Particular Goods	**Article 1828.**
Capítulo IV – Acreedores de primera clase	**Chapter IV** - First-Class Creditors	**Article 1829.**
Capítulo V – Acreedores de segunda clase	**Chapter V** - Second-Class Creditors	**Articles 1830 through 1831.**
Capítulo VI – Acreedores de tercera clase	**Chapter VI** - Third-Class Creditors	**Article 1831.**
Capítulo VII – Acreedores de cuarta clase	**Chapter VII** - Fourth-Class Creditors	**Articles 1832 through 1833.**

Libro Quinto - De las diversas especies de contratos
Book 5 - The Various Types of Contracts

Título Primero - De los contratos preliminares
Title 1 - Preliminary Contracts

Capítulo I – De la promesa para contratar	**Chapter I** - The Promise to Enter Into a Contract	**Articles 1834 through 1838.**
Capítulo II – De la opción	**Chapter II** - Options	**Articles 1839 through 1844.**
Capítulo III – De la carta intención	**Chapter III** - Letters of Intent	**Articles 1845 through 1849.**

Título Segundo - De la compraventa
Title 2 - Sales Contracts

Capítulo I – Disposiciones generales	**Chapter I** - General Provisions	**Articles 1850 through 1862.**
Capítulo II – De la materia de la compraventa	**Chapter II** - Subject Matter of the Sales Contract	**Articles 1863 through 1867.**
Capítulo III – De las partes en la compraventa	**Chapter III** - The Parties to the Sales Contract	**Articles 1868 through 1870.**
Capítulo IV – De las obligaciones del vendedor	**Chapter IV** - The Seller's Obligations	**Articles 1871 through 1882.**

Spanish	English	Articles
Capítulo V – De las obligaciones del comprador	**Chapter V** - The Buyer's Obligations	**Articles 1883 through 1891.**
Capítulo VI – De algunas modalidades del contrato de compraventa	**Chapter VI** - Characteristics of Sales Contracts	**Articles 1892 through 1906.**
Capítulo VII – De la forma del contrato de compraventa	**Chapter VII** - The Form of the Sales Contract	**Articles 1907 through 1908.**
Título Tercero - De la permuta	**Title 3 - Barter Transactions**	
No hay capítulos	No chapters	**Articles 1909 through 1913.**
Título Cuarto - De las donaciones	**Title 4 - Donations**	
Capítulo I – De las donaciones en general	**Chapter I** - Donations in General	**Articles 1914 through 1940.**
Capítulo II – De las personas que pueden recibir donaciones	**Chapter II** - Persons That Can Receive Donations	**Articles 1941 through 1942.**
Capítulo III – De la revocación y reducción de las donaciones	**Chapter III** - Cancellation and Reduction of Donations	**Articles 1943 through 1965.**
Título Quinto - Del mutuo	**Title 5 - Consumption Loans**	
	A **consumption loan** is a loan of personal goods intended to be consumed by the borrower, and to be returned to the lender in kind and quantity. For example, a loan of corn, tequila, or money, which is meant to be used or consumed, and is to be replaced by different corn, tequila, or money.	
Capítulo I – Del mutuo simple	**Chapter I** - The Simple Consumption Loan	**Articles 1966 through 1973.**
Capítulo II – Del mutuo con interés	**Chapter II** - Consumption Loans With Interest	**Articles 1974 through 1979.**

Título Sexto – Del arrendamiento	Title 6 - Leases	
Capítulo I – Disposiciones generales	**Chapter I** - General Provisions	**Articles 1980 through 1994.**
Capítulo II – De los derechos y obligaciones del arrendador	**Chapter II** - Rights and Obligations of the Lessor [person granting the lease]	**Articles 1995 through 2004.**
Capítulo III – De los derechos y obligaciones del arrendatario	**Chapter III** - Rights and Obligations of the Lessee [person to whom lease is granted]	**Articles 2005 through 2022.**
Capítulo IV – Del arrendamiento de bienes inmuebles destinados a fines agropecuarios	**Chapter IV** - Leasing Real Estate Destined for Agricultural Use	**Articles 2023 through 2063.**
Capítulo V – Del arrendamiento de bienes muebles	**Chapter V** - Leasing of Goods	**Articles 2064 through 2079.**
Capítulo VI – Del arrendamiento con prestación de servicios y derecho a uso de áreas comunes	**Chapter VI** - Leasing *Property* With Provision of Services and Right to Use Common Areas	**Articles 2080 through 2090.**
Capítulo VII – Del arrendamiento de promoción y exhibición	**Chapter VII** - Leasing of Promotion and Exhibit *Space*	**Articles 2091 through 2096.**
Capítulo VIII – Del arrendamiento con opción a compra	**Chapter VIII** - Leasing With the Option to Buy	**Articles 2097 through 2113.**
Capítulo IX – Del arrendamiento de vehículos automotores	**Chapter IX** - Leasing of Automobiles	**Articles 2114 through 2128.**
Capítulo X – Del arrendamiento de membresías de clubes	**Chapter X** - Leasing of Club Memberships	Allowing another to use your club membership for a fee by contract. **Articles 2129 through 2135.**
Capítulo XI – Del subarriendo	**Chapter XI** - Sub-Leasing	**Articles 2136 through 2139.**
Capítulo XII – Del modo de terminar el arrendamiento	**Chapter XII** - Ways to Terminate a Lease	**Articles 2140 through 2146.**
Título Septimo - Del comodato	Title 7 - Commodatum	
No hay capítulos	No chapters	**Commodatum** is a legal term meaning the grant of free and temporary use of a fixed asset. **Articles 2147 through 2166.**

Title 11 - Metayage System

The Metayage System is a legal term for a farm partnership allowing cultivation of the land for an owner by someone else who gets a proportion of the produce.

Chapter I - General Provisions — **Articles 2333 through 2347.**

Chapter II - Sharecropping — **Articles 2348 through 2354.**

Chapter III - Farm Partnership With Animals — Involves animals, fish, or bees instead of crops. **Articles 2355 through 2366.**

Título Decimoprimero - De la aparcería

Capítulo I – Disposiciones generales

Capítulo II – De la aparcería agrícola

Capítulo III – De la aparcería animal

Title 12 - Aleatory Contracts

An aleatory contract is one whose outcome is dependent on luck, chance, or uncertainty.

Chapter I - Games and Wagers — **Articles 2367 through 2376.**

Chapter II - Life Annuities — **Articles 2377 through 2393.**

Chapter III - Futures Contracts — **Articles 2394 through 2400.**

Título Decimosegundo - De los contratos aleatorios

Capítulo I – Del juego y de la apuesta

Capítulo II – De la renta vitalicia

Capítulo III – De la compra de esperanza

Title 13 - The Guaranty

A guaranty is an agreement where a person assures payment of another's debts or obligations. For example, co-signing a loan.

Chapter I - The Guaranty in General — **Articles 2401 through 2422.**

Chapter II - The Effects of the Guaranty On the Guarantor and the Creditor — **Articles 2423 through 2437.**

Chapter III - The Effects of the Guaranty On the Guarantor and a Purchase on Credit — **Articles 2438 through 2446.**

Chapter IV - The Effects of the Guaranty On the Co-Guarantors — **Articles 2447 through 2455.**

Chapter V - Terminating the Guaranty — **Articles 2456 through 2463.**

Chapter VI - Legal or Judicial Guaranties — **Articles 2464 through 2472.**

Título Decimotercero - De la fianza

Capítulo I – De la fianza en general

Capítulo II – De los efectos de la fianza entre el fiador y el acreedor

Capítulo III – De los efectos de la fianza entre el fiador y el fiado

Capítulo IV – De los efectos de la fianza entre los cofiadores

Capítulo V – De la extinción de la fianza

Capítulo VI – De la fianza legal o judicial

Title 14 - Collateral — A pledge of security on a debt.		**Título Decimocuarto - De la prenda**
Chapter I - General Provisions	Articles 2473 through 2487.	Capítulo I – Disposiciones generales
Chapter II - Fruit as Collateral	Articles 2488 through 2490.	Capítulo II – De la prenda sobre frutos
Chapter III - Collateral Relating to Financing and Negotiable Instruments	Articles 2491 through 2496.	Capítulo III – De la prenda sobre créditos o títulos de crédito
Chapter IV - Rights and Obligations of the Creditor and a Pignorative Debtor — A **pignorative debtor** is a property owner who allows someone who has lent him money the right to use and enjoy his property until the debt is paid.	Articles 2497 through 2503.	Capítulo IV – Derechos y obligaciones del acreedor y deudor pignoraticios
Chapter V - Terminating Collateral	Articles 2504 through 2516.	Capítulo V – De la extinción de la prenda
Title 15 - Mortgages		**Título Decimoquinto - De la hipoteca**
Chapter I - Mortgages in General	Articles 2517 through 2547.	Capítulo I – De la hipoteca en general
Chapter II - The Voluntary Mortgage	Articles 2548 through 2562.	Capítulo II – De la hipoteca voluntaria
Chapter III - The Compulsory Mortgage — Mortgage contract imposed by law to ensure payment of creditors or the administration of certain goods.	Articles 2563 through 2570.	Capítulo III – De la hipoteca necesaria
Chapter IV - Common Provisions for the Various Types of Mortgages	Articles 2571 through 2579.	Capítulo IV – Disposiciones comunes a las diversas clases de hipotecas
Chapter V - Termination of a Mortgage	Articles 2580 through 2591.	Capítulo V – De la extinción de las hipotecas
Title 16 - Arbitration Agreements		**Título Decimosexto - Contrato de compromiso arbitral**
Chapter I - General Provisions	Articles 2592 through 2604.	Capítulo I – Disposiciones generales
Chapter II - Designation and Acceptance of Arbitrators	Articles 2605 through 2618.	Capítulo II – De la designación y aceptación de árbitros
Chapter III - Obligations of the Parties to an Arbitration	Articles 2619 through 2623.	Capítulo III – De las obligaciones de los comprometientes

Spanish	English	Articles
Capítulo IV – Modalidades del contrato de compromiso arbitral	**Chapter IV** - Nature of the Arbitration Agreement	**Articles 2624 through 2628.**
Capítulo V – De la cláusula compromisoria	**Chapter V** - Arbitration Clauses	Can be put in any contract or the establishing documents of companies, associations, and other legal entities. **Articles 2629 through 2632.**
Título Decimoseptimo - De las transacciones	**Title 17 - Transactions**	A **transaction** is a civil law term for a contract by which the parties end a current dispute (or prevent a future one) by making mutual concessions. **Articles 2633 through 2651.**
No hay capítulos	**No Chapters**	
Libro Sexto - De las sucesiones	**Book 6 - Succession [and Inheritance]**	
Título Primero - Disposiciones preliminares	**Title 1 - Preliminary Provisions**	
No hay capítulos	No chapters	**Articles 2652 through 2665.**
Título Segundo - De la sucesión por testamento	**Title 2 - Inheritance by Will**	
Capítulo I – De los testamentos en general	**Chapter I** - Wills in General	**Articles 2666 through 2675.**
Capítulo II – De la capacidad para testar	**Chapter II** - The Capacity to Make a Will	**Articles 2676 through 2679.**
Capítulo III – De las condiciones que pueden ponerse en los testamentos	**Chapter III** - The Conditions That Can Be Placed in a Will	**Articles 2680 through 2703.**
Capítulo IV – De los testamentos inoficiosos	**Chapter III** - Inofficious Wills	An **inofficious will** is one contrary to moral obligation and natural affection, such as when a child is disinherited. **Articles 2704 through 2708.**
Capítulo V – De la institución de heredero	**Chapter V** - Appointment of an Heir	**Articles 2709 through 2721.**
Capítulo VI – De los legados	**Chapter VI** - Beneficiaries	**Articles 2722 through 2801.**

Chapter VII - Substitutions **Capítulo VII** – De las sustituciones	**Substitution** is when different beneficiaries inherit under different conditions – for example, if one dies first. **Articles 2802 through 2813.**
Chapter VIII - Nullification, Revocation, and Expiry of Wills **Capítulo VIII** – De la nulidad, revocación y caducidad de los testamentos	**Articles 2814 through 2828.**

Title 3 - Types of Wills

Título Tercero - De la forma de los testamentos

Chapter I - General Provisions **Capítulo I** – Disposiciones generales	**Articles 2829 through 2840.**
Chapter II - Public Open Will **Capítulo II** – Del testamento público abierto	Dictated before a *notario* with two witnesses. Publicly registered. **Articles 2841 through 2847.**
Chapter III - Public Closed Will **Capítulo III** – Del testamento público cerrado	Written by person making the Will (or someone else at his direction) by mechanical or electronic means, and presented to a *notario* who bears witness that this is the person's will. Publicly registered. **Articles 2848 through 2872.**
Chapter IV - Holographic Will **Capítulo IV** – Del testamento ológrafo	Only available to the elderly. Will is handwritten, signed, and fingerprinted by the person making the Will without witness signatures. Two copies, one publicly registered. **Articles 2873 through 2887.**
Chapter V - Private Will **Capítulo V** – Del testamento privado	Allowed only when it's impossible or very difficult to go before a *notario*. Not publicly registered. **Articles 2888 through 2899.**
Chapter VI - Military and Maritime Wills **Capítulo VI** – Del testamento militar y marítimo	**Articles 2900 through 2904.**

Spanish	English	Articles
Capítulo VII – El testamento hecho fuera del Estado	**Chapter VII** - A Will Made Outside of the State *of Jalisco* [but within México]	**Article 2905.**
Capítulo VIII – El testamento hecho en país extranjero	**Chapter VIII** - A Will Made in a Foreign Country [by a Mexican]	**Articles 2906 through 2907.**
Título Cuarto - De la sucesión legítima	**Title 4 - Legal Succession [inheritance rules]**	
Capítulo I – Disposiciones generales	**Chapter I** - General Provisions	**Articles 2908 through 2914.**
Capítulo II – De la sucesión de los descendientes	**Chapter II** - *Inheritance* by *Direct* Descendents [children of deceased]	**Articles 2915 through 2920.**
Capítulo III – De la sucesión de los ascendientes	**Chapter III** - *Inheritance* by *Direct* Antecedents [parents of deceased]	**Articles 2921 through 2929.**
Capítulo IV – De la sucesión del cónyuge	**Chapter IV** - *Inheritance* by the Spouse [of the deceased]	**Articles 2930 through 2935.**
Capítulo V – De la sucesión de los colaterales	**Chapter V** - *Inheritance* by the *Indirect Relatives* [brothers, cousins, and so on]	**Articles 2936 through 2940.**
Capítulo VI – De la sucesión de los concubinos	**Chapter VI** - *Inheritance* by a Cohabitational Partner	A **cohabitational partner** is a partner in a non-matrimonial union. **Article 2941.**
Capítulo VII – De la sucesión de la Beneficencia Pública	**Chapter VII** - *Inheritance* for the Public Benefit	If none of the above heirs exist, and there are no other beneficiaries, the estate passes to a state social welfare agency. **Article 2942.**
Título Quinto - Disposiciones comunes a las sucesiones testamentaria y legítima	**Title 5 - Common Provisions for Inheritance by Wills and by Law**	
Capítulo I – De las precauciones que deben adoptarse cuando la viuda quede encinta	**Chapter I** - Precautions That Should Be Adopted When a Widow Becomes Pregnant	**Articles 2943 through 2953.**
Capítulo II – De la capacidad para heredar	**Chapter II** - The Capacity to Inherit	**Articles 2954 through 2983.**

Capítulo	Chapter	Articles
	Requirement to provide necessities.	Articles 2984 through 2989.
Capítulo III – De las cargas alimentarias	Chapter III - The Onus of Maintenance	Articles 2984 through 2989.
Capítulo IV – De la apertura y transmisión de la herencia	Chapter IV - The Recital and Transmittal of the Bequest	Articles 2990 through 2993.
Capítulo V – De la aceptación y de la repudiación de la herencia	Chapter V - Acceptance and Rejection of a Bequest	Articles 2994 through 3019.
Capítulo VI – De los albaceas e interventores	Chapter VI - Executors and Trustees	Articles 3020 through 3096.
Capítulo VII – Del inventario y de la liquidación de la herencia	Chapter VII - Inventory and the Closing Out of the Estate	Articles 3097 through 3108.
Capítulo VIII – De la partición	Chapter VIII - Division [of the estate]	Articles 3109 through 3122.
Capítulo IX – De los efectos de la partición	Chapter IX - Effects of Division	Articles 3123 through 3131.
Capítulo X – De la rescisión y nulidad de las particiones	Chapter X - Cancellation and Invalidity of the Division	Articles 3132 through 3134.

PART 3 – The Jalisco Condo Law

Civil Code of the State of Jalisco Book 3 – Title 6 Articles 1001 – 1038

Relevance to condominiums

Condominiums established after 1995 are incorporated into a *régimen de Condominio* (condominium regime) and governed by a section of the Jalisco Civil Code. This regime contains all the elements of a condo owners' association, but **is not an association**. Before 1995, the condo regime was regulated by a separate condo law (outside of the Civil Code).

In 1995, the condominium regime also became a separate legal entity (see ***Part 6 – Legal Entities*** for more information on this concept), with full legal rights to act on behalf of the titleholders of the property within the condo. Before 1995, this was not the case, and a civil association was needed to legally represent the condo regime.

Condos established before 1995 are still regulated by whatever condo law was in effect at the time the condo was set up, unless, sometime after 1995, the condo regime was re-established under the new law.

It's important to understand that an association and a condo regime are two separate and different legal entities, and are governed by separate and different laws (see ***Part 10 – Civil Associations*** for laws governing associations).

The section of the Civil Code translated here contains the **entire condominium legislation**, and is essential to the administration of a condo regime established after 1995.

Versions of Laws Used

Codes and laws are living documents that are amended frequently by the level of government that issued them.

This section contains an excerpt from the *Código Civil del Estado de Jalisco* (Civil Code of the State of Jalisco), that took effect on **September 14, 1995**, and was last amended on ***December 20, 2014***.

Sections of the Laws Used

The excerpt from the Jalisco Civil Code translated in this section is *Libro Tercero – Título Sexto*:

> *Libro Tercero* (Book Three) is titled *"De los bienes, su propiedad y sus diferentes manifestaciones"* (Property, Its Ownership, and Its Different Forms).

> *Título Sexto* (Title Six) is titled *"Del Condominio"* (The condominium).

Definitions

These are terms used throughout the English translation in this section:

condominium: means the condominium as a legal entity incorporated under a *régimen de condominio* (condominium regime), and referred to in the Civil Code using the term "*condominio*".

When the condominium's physical property (all of the private and common property) is referred to by "*unidad condominal*" in the Code, the phrase "**condominium unit**" is used in this translation to make this distinction clear.

private unit: means an individual lot or apartment. This is referred to in the Civil Code using the term "*unidad privativa*".

titleholder: means the titleholder(s) of a private unit who also owns a percentage of the common property. This is referred to in the Civil Code using the term "*condómino*".

Assembly: means "**Assembly of Titleholders**," and is the owners of the condominium gathered at an ordinary or extraordinary assembly to make decisions on budgets and fees, the make-up of the condo's administration, by-law changes, and other major condominium issues. This is referred to in the Civil Code using the term "*asamblea de condóminos*".

Administrator: means the person, company, or other legal entity appointed by the titleholders at an annual ordinary assembly to carry out the administrative duties outlined in **Chapter II** of this section of the Code and the condominium's by-laws. This is referred to in the Civil Code using the term "*administrador*".

Administrative Council: means the group of owners or occupants elected by the titleholders at an annual ordinary assembly to carry out the administrative duties outlined in **Chapter III** of this section of the Code and the condominium's by-laws. This is referred to in the Civil Code using the term "*Consejo de administración*," and is often translated (inaccurately) by foreigners as "**Board of Directors**".

| CÓDIGO CIVIL DEL ESTADO DE JALISCO | CIVIL CODE OF THE STATE OF JALISCO |

CÓDIGO CIVIL DEL ESTADO DE JALISCO

LIBRO TERCERO

TÍTULO SEXTO – DEL CONDOMINIO

CAPÍTULO I – Prevenciones generales

Artículo 1001. Condominio es el régimen jurídico que integra las modalidades y limitaciones al dominio de un predio o edificación y la reglamentación de su uso y destino, para su aprovechamiento conjunto y simultáneo.

Los titulares de la propiedad en condominio reciben la denominación de **condóminos. La titularidad** puede referirse a un espacio o a un uso y bienes determinados en forma exclusiva, cuyo aprovechamiento y disposición es libre, que se denominan áreas o bienes privativos; además **la titularidad exclusiva** está referida porcentualmente a las áreas y bienes de uso común, los que no podrán ser objeto de acción divisoria y son inseparables de la propiedad individual.

El conjunto de áreas y bienes privativos, con las áreas, instalaciones y bienes de uso común, que hacen posible su aprovechamiento por un grupo de titulares, se denomina **unidad condominal**.

El conjunto de bienes cuyo aprovechamiento y libre disposición corresponden a un condómino, se denomina **unidad privativa**.

CIVIL CODE OF THE STATE OF JALISCO

BOOK THREE

TITLE SIX – THE CONDOMINIUM

CHAPTER I – General Provisions [The Condominium]

Article 1001.- *"Condominio"* **[referred to as a "condominium" in this translation]** is a legal regime **[system]** that incorporates the forms and limitations of the *rights to use, control, and own* a property or buildings, *with* the regulation of their use and purpose, and for their joint and simultaneous enjoyment.

The title holders of property in a condominium are called *"condóminos"* **[referred to as "titleholders" in this translation]. Title** refers to the exclusive ownership of an area or to an exclusive use of property, that has been designated a private area or property, including the sole right to use, enjoy, and freely dispose of such property. In addition, the **exclusive title** is related proportionally to the common areas and properties. It cannot be divided, and is inseparable from *the title to* the individual property.

The set of private areas and properties, together with the common areas, facilities, and properties available for use by a group of title holders, are called the **condominium unit**.

The set of properties, whose use and the right to freely dispose of them belong to a titleholder, are called a **private unit**.

Artículo 1002. En atención al funcionamiento y aprovechamiento de los elementos comunes, por una o varias unidades condominales, se clasifican en **condominio simple** o **condominio compuesto**.

El condominio es **simple**, cuando las áreas comunes y sus obras de infraestructura y equipamiento, corresponden a una sola unidad condominal.

El condominio es **compuesto**, cuando una parte de sus áreas comunes y obras de infraestructura y equipamiento, son aprovechadas por los titulares de dos o más unidades condominales, que coexisten en un mismo predio.

Artículo 1003. En atención a la distribución de las áreas comunes y privativas, respecto al predio y las edificaciones, el condominio se clasifica en **horizontal**, **vertical** y **mixto**.

El condominio es **horizontal**, cuando a cada condómino le corresponde como área privativa una fracción o lote del predio, con su edificación e instalaciones.

El condominio es **vertical**, cuando la totalidad del predio es bien común y una misma estructura arquitectónica, se divide en áreas privativas.

El condominio es **mixto**, cuando concurren las condiciones a que se refieren los párrafos anteriores, para los condominios horizontal y vertical.

Article 1002.- In relation to the operation and use of the common elements by one or more condominium units, condominiums are classified as **simple** or **compound**.

A condominium is **simple** when the common areas, infrastructure, and equipment are contained within a single condominium unit.

A condominium is **compound** when part of its common areas, infrastructure, and equipment are used by the titleholders of two or more condominium units that coexist on the same property.

Article 1003.- In relation to the distribution of the common and the private areas, in terms of the property and buildings, a condominium is classified as **horizontal**, **vertical**, or **mixed**.

A condominium is **horizontal** when a lot or fraction of the property, along with its buildings and facilities, belongs to each titleholder as a private area **[such as individual houses and lots in a gated community]**.

A condominium is **vertical** when the entire premises are *designated as* common property, and a single architectural structure is divided into private areas **[such as a block of condo apartments]**.

A condominium is **mixed** when the conditions referred to in the previous paragraphs for *both* horizontal and vertical condominiums are met.

Artículo 1004. En atención a su uso, al condominio le corresponderá la categoría que determinen las normas urbanísticas de zonificación, como son: habitacional; alojamiento temporal; comercios y servicios; oficinas administrativas; abastos, almacenamientos y talleres especiales; manufacturas y usos industriales.

El **condominio de servicios municipales**, es aquel que está destinado a complementar el equipamiento urbano de una comunidad.

Artículo 1005. Todo condominio habitacional, simple o compuesto, tendrá una extensión máxima de diez hectáreas o una población que no exceda de dos mil quinientos habitantes. Estos límites de extensión territorial y de población podrán incrementarse hasta veinte por ciento, cuando por las características del lugar o de las funciones a desarrollar, de conformidad con las normas de urbanización aplicables, se demuestre la necesidad de zonas de mayor dimensión o población.

Los condominios para usos o destinos distintos del habitacional tendrán la extensión máxima que determinen las normas municipales de zonificación.

Artículo 1006. Para constituir el **régimen de condominio** respecto de un predio o edificación, se requiere que quien tenga su libre disposición, solicite y obtenga autorización del municipio donde se localice el inmueble y lo formalice en escritura pública, en la que se hará constar de manera clara, lo siguiente:

I. Los antecedentes de propiedad y en su caso el título que origine la libre disposición;

Article 1004.- In relation to its use, the condominium will fit into a specific use category determined by municipal zoning codes, such as: residential; temporary accommodations; business and services; administrative offices; wholesalers, warehouses, specialist workshops, and manufacturing and industrial uses.

A **Municipal Services condominium** is one that is intended to supplement the urban development of a community **[such as social or public housing and cemeteries]**.

Article 1005.- All residential condominiums, simple or compound, must have a maximum area of ten hectares **[about 25 acres]**, or a population that does not exceed two thousand five hundred **[2,500]** residents. These territorial and population limits can be increased by up to twenty percent **[20%]**, when, because of the characteristics of the place or purpose of the development, the necessity for zones of larger size or population has been demonstrated in accordance with applicable town planning codes.

Condominiums intended for nonresidential use will have a maximum size determined by the municipal town planning codes.

Article 1006.- To establish a **condominium regime** for a property or a building, whoever has free title must ask for and obtain authorisation from the municipality where the real estate is located, and formalise *its establishment* in a publicly registered document, that must clearly state the following:

I. The history of the properties title and, as required, the title from which the ability to freely dispose of the property originates;

II. La ubicación, medidas y linderos del predio; y en su caso, las concesiones para el aprovechamiento de aguas, playas, esteros e islas del dominio público de la nación. Además cuando sea parte de un condominio compuesto, la noticia de ello, así como el porcentaje que en áreas comunes, derechos y obligaciones le corresponden;

III. Una descripción general de las construcciones y obras de infraestructura, así como del equipamiento urbano que exista; y la calidad de los materiales que se empleen en su edificación;

IV. Una descripción individual de cada unidad privativa que se genere, indicándose su número ordinal, su situación, medidas, linderos, clase de material utilizado, servicios a que se tenga derecho, así como el porcentaje que le corresponda sobre los elementos comunes. Además si existen áreas de servicios separadas físicamente de la unidad privativa, se indicará con toda precisión cuáles son éstas;

V. Cuando el área de servicios correspondiente a la unidad privativa esté separada físicamente de los otros bienes de uso exclusivo, se referirá con la nomenclatura que sirva de identificación y se hará también una descripción general de la misma, con sus medidas y linderos. Estas áreas de servicios, se consideran en forma accesoria y por ello, pueden transmitirse el uso o propiedad entre los condóminos, fijándose en estos casos la proporción porcentual sobre los elementos comunes;

II. The location, dimensions, and boundaries of the property, and, as required, the concessions for water rights, beaches, estuaries, and islands **which are part of** the nation's public **heritage**. In addition, when it is part of a compound condominium, proof of this **[being part of a compound condominium]** as well as the percentage **interest** in the common areas, and its corresponding rights and obligations;

III. A general description of the buildings and infrastructure, as well as the existing municipal services; and the quality of materials that are used in their construction;

IV. A separate description of each private unit, showing its numeric designation, location, dimensions, boundaries, grade of materials used, services to which it has a right, as well as the percentage **interest** in the common elements belonging to this private unit **[the unit's condo rights]**. In addition, if there are service areas which are separate from the private unit, these must be precisely indicated;

V. When a private unit's service area is physically separated from the other exclusive-use property, this area must be clearly identified, and a general description must be provided with its dimensions and boundaries. These service areas are considered as supplementary **[to the private unit]**, and, for that reason, their use or ownership can be transferred between titleholders, with special attention being paid, in this case, to the proportional percentage of the common elements;

VI. Una descripción de las áreas comunes, señalándose su situación, medidas, linderos, partes de que se componga, obras de infraestructura, equipamiento y mobiliario afectos a ellas, su uso y cuando fuere posible, su marca comercial e inventarios. Exclusivamente y para prestación de servicios comunes, se podrán considerar en el acto de constitución del régimen de propiedad en condominio, o con posterioridad a este acto, cuando se convenga en su incorporación por su evidente utilidad, áreas separadas físicamente de la unidad condominal, haciéndose la descripción correspondiente;

VII. La clasificación del condominio, de acuerdo a sus aspectos de funcionamiento y aprovechamiento de elementos comunes; la distribución de las áreas comunes y privativas; su uso y destino;

VIII. La referencia de haberse obtenido la autorización para constituir el régimen de condominio, indicando su extensión o población, así como los dictámenes, autorizaciones o licencias que correspondan, en materia de urbanización;

IX. La información relativa a las licencias y permisos de construcción. Cuando sea parte de un condominio compuesto del que exista consejo de administración, su aprobación aceptando que el proyecto de la unidad condominal cumple con los objetivos y acata los criterios de diseño y las restricciones generales de condominio. Cuando esté ya concluida la edificación, el certificado de habitabilidad.

VI. A description of the common areas, showing their location, dimensions, boundaries, parts comprising them, infrastructure, equipment and furnishings belonging to them, their use, and, when possible, their brand names and quantities. Exclusively, and for providing common services, areas physically separated from the condominium unit, along with their corresponding description, can be considered in the establishment of the condominium regime, or after it is established, when it is agreed to incorporate them due to their obvious benefit;

VII. The classification of the condominium, according to its operating characteristics and use of common elements, the distribution of the common and private areas, and their use and purpose;

VIII. Proof of having obtained the authorisation to establish the condominium regime, showing its size and population, as well as any opinions, authorisations, or licenses applicable to town planning matters;

IX. Information relating to the licenses and permits for construction. When it is part of a compound condominium which has an existing Administrative Council, **the Council's** approval agreeing that the condominium unit project fulfils the objectives of, and complies with, the design criteria and the general restrictions of the **compound** condominium. **If** the construction is already finished, **attach** the occupancy certificate.

En su caso, cuando la edificación sea entregada a los condóminos en obra negra, para que cada uno de ellos haga las adaptaciones correspondientes, así se hará constar en las certificaciones que se expidan por las autoridades;

X. La referencia a las garantías que constituye el afectante al régimen de condominio, ante la autoridad municipal de la ubicación del inmueble, para responder tanto por la terminación de las obras, como por la calidad de las mismas;

XI. El reglamento interior del condominio de manera particular regulará:

    a) Los derechos y obligaciones de los condóminos, que serán proporcionales al porcentaje que les correspondan sobre los elementos comunes;

    b) Las facultades de los órganos de administración y de gobierno;

    c) La formación de los fondos de reserva y en su caso, el establecimiento de comités para asuntos particulares que coadyuven con el consejo de administración, los que pueden tener autonomía financiera;

    d) El establecimiento de las bases para el pago de las cuotas de mantenimiento, conservación y creación de fondos de reserva que se incurra;

    e) El establecimiento de criterios para la restricción de giros en cuanto a la cantidad y de actividades afines, mismos que deberá respetar el ayuntamiento al autorizar las licencias respectivas;

In the event that the building is **turned over** to the titleholders in an unfinished form, so that each of them makes corresponding alterations, this fact must be indicated in all the certifications issued by the authorities;

X. Proof of the guarantees **[in the form of a bond]** affecting the condominium regime, **made** before the municipal authority where the real estate is located, to **guarantee** the quality and completion of the work;

XI. The condominium's by-laws, that must, in particular, regulate:

    a) The rights and obligations of the titleholders, which must be proportional to the percentage in the common elements that corresponds to **each owner**;

    b) The authority of the administrative bodies and governments;

    c) The formation of reserve funds and, as the case may be, the establishment of committees for particular purposes that collaborate with the Administrative Council; these can be financially independent **[the committees]**;

    d) The establishment of the basis for the payment of fees for repairs and maintenance expenses that are incurred, and for the creation of reserve funds;

    e) The establishment of criteria for the restriction of business in terms of quantity and of related activities, which must be respected by the municipal government when authorising the relevant licenses;

f) La instancia y el procedimiento para resolver conflictos entre los condóminos;

g) Los casos y condiciones en que pueda ser modificado el propio reglamento; y

h) La transformación y extinción del condominio;

XII. La forma en que los condóminos responderán del pago de las cuotas establecidas en el **artículo 1026**; y

XIII. Se agregarán los planos de zonificación del condominio, los planos generales de la edificación y los de las unidades privativas.

La escritura constitutiva del régimen de condominio deberá inscribirse en el Registro Público de la Propiedad.

Artículo 1007. Son bienes comunes, atendiendo a su clasificación, como a su edificación, siempre que sean de uso general:

I. Las obras de cimentación;

II. Las obras de infraestructura y equipamiento urbano;

III. Los pórticos, puertas, corredores, escaleras, pasillos y patios;

IV. Los espacios de recreación y jardines;

V. Los estacionamientos al público, las rúas y andadores;

---

f) The application and procedures to resolve disputes between titleholders;

g) The circumstances and conditions under which the by-laws can be modified; and

h) The transformation **[changing it to another form of property]** and termination of the condominium.

XII. The way in which the titleholders must submit payment of the fees established in **Article 1026**; and

XIII. Attach to it the zoning plans of the condominium unit, the general plans of construction **[of the common property]**, and those of the private units.

The *escritura constitutiva* (establishing document of the condominium regime) must be registered in the "*Registro Público de la Propiedad*" (Public Registry of Property).

Article 1007.- Common property, according to its classification and its construction, providing it is for general use, ***includes***:

I. Foundation works;

II. Infrastructure and municipal services;

III. Porches, doors, paths, stairs, corridors, and patios;

IV. Recreational areas and gardens;

V. Public parking, streets, and walkways;

VI. Los locales de administración, almacenes de mobiliario destinado al condominio, como las bodegas, los locales destinados al alojamiento de porteros, vigilantes, jardineros, y servidumbre;

VII. Los ductos y postería para servicios de suministro como gas, y energía eléctrica;

VIII. Los cableados para servicios telefónicos, de televisión por cable y conexiones a antenas para captar señales de radio y televisión;

IX. Los fosos, pozos, tinacos, cisternas, ductos de aguas pluviales y drenaje;

X. Las plantas de tratamiento de aguas residuales;

XI. Los pozos de absorción de aguas pluviales;

XII. Los ductos de desagüe y de calefacción;

XIII. Los ascensores, escaleras eléctricas y montacargas;

XIV. Los muros de carga y las azoteas; y

XV. Los demás que por su naturaleza y destino tengan ese fin.

El administrador llevará un inventario completo y actualizado de todos los bienes muebles e inmuebles, de uso general pertenecientes al condominio.

VI. Administration offices, storage areas for condominium furniture, and premises intended to house: doormen, security guards, gardeners, and employees;

VII. Ducts and utility pedestals for services such as gas and electrical power;

VIII. Wiring for telephone, cable television, and connections to antennas for radio and television;

IX. Ditches, wells, water containers [such as *tinacos*], cisterns [such as *aljibes*], and water pipes for rain water and drainage;

X. Waste water treatment plants;

XI. Absorption wells for rain water;

XII. Pipes for water drainage and heating;

XIII. Elevators, escalators, and freight elevators;

XIV. Retaining walls and terrace roofs; and

XV. Anything else that, by its nature and intent, has the same purpose.

The Administrator must make a complete and updated inventory of all furniture and buildings of common use belonging to the condominium.

Artículo 1008. Cada condómino podrá servirse de los bienes comunes y gozar de los servicios e instalaciones generales, conforme a su naturaleza y destino ordinario, sin restringir o hacer más oneroso el derecho de los demás.

Los derechos de cada condómino en los bienes comunes son esenciales a sus derechos de propiedad individual, por ello cualquier afectación o disposición de la misma, se entiende referida a los bienes comunes.

El condómino que no haga uso de su propiedad o de algunos bienes comunes, no quedará exento de las obligaciones que le competan como tal.

Para conservar la armonía del condominio, cada vecino procurará hacer uso de su unidad privativa sin afectar la tranquilidad de los demás condóminos, ni destinarla a usos contrarios a los señalados en la escritura constitutiva.

Artículo 1009. Para la realización de obras en bienes e instalaciones generales, se observarán las siguientes reglas:

I. Las obras de conservación se efectuarán por determinación del administrador, siguiendo instrucciones permanentes o precisas del Consejo de Administración y sin necesidad de acuerdo de los condóminos, con cargo al fondo de gastos de mantenimiento y administración;

Article 1008.- Each titleholder can use the common property, and enjoy the services and general facilities, according to their nature and intended use, **but** without restricting the rights of others or making these rights more difficult **[for the others to exercise]**.

The rights of each titleholder in the common property are **integral** to their rights of individual property ownership, **therefore**, any acquisition or disposal of **a titleholder's private property** is understood to **also** refer to **their** common property **rights**.

A titleholder who does not use their property, or part of the common property, is not relieved from the obligations incumbent upon them **[such as paying fees]**.

To maintain the harmony of the condominium, each neighbour must try to use their private unit without affecting the tranquillity of the other titleholders, nor can they use it in ways contrary to **the uses** indicated in the registered establishing document for the condominium.

Article 1009.- In carrying out work on the general property and facilities **[common property]**, the following rules must be observed:

I. Maintenance work must only take place at the determination of the Administrator, following established or precise instructions of the Administrative Council, without requiring the agreement of the titleholders, and must be paid for with the funds for maintenance and administration expenses;

II. El administrador, deberá hacer efectivas las garantías que en su caso otorguen el constituyente del condominio, o los contratistas que realizaron las obras;

III. Las obras de mejoramiento se harán previo acuerdo de condóminos tomado en asamblea extraordinaria.

Dichas obras serán dirigidas en su ejecución por el administrador, con la vigilancia del consejo de administración o cuando se nombre una comisión específica para ello, bajo responsabilidad de la misma.

No se realizarán obras que atenten a la estabilidad e infraestructura del edificio, o que menoscaben la seguridad o comodidad del condominio, así como que impidan permanentemente el uso de una parte o un servicio común aunque sólo sea a un condómino; a no ser que éste consienta y sea indemnizado proporcionalmente por los demás; y

IV. Las reparaciones urgentes a bienes o instalaciones comunes cuyo desperfecto ponga en peligro la seguridad de los condóminos, la integridad del inmueble o que impidan el buen funcionamiento de los servicios comunes, deberán ser efectuadas por el administrador en tiempo prudente,

II. The Administrator must enforce the guarantees that, as the case may be, are given by the ***person establishing*** the condominium, or by the contractors carrying out ***the*** work;

III. Improvements **[work beyond repairs and maintenance, such as adding something that didn't previously exist]** require prior agreement of the titleholders in an Extraordinary Assembly.

These ***improvements*** must be supervised by the Administrator, and monitored by the Administrative Council, or be under the responsibility of a committee, when a specific committee is ***created*** for this work.

Work cannot be carried out that undermines the stability and infrastructure of a building, or that reduces the security or comfort of the condominium, or that permanently impedes the use of a part ***of the common property*** or a common service, even if this only ***affects*** one titleholder, unless ***that titleholder*** consents to this, and is compensated proportionally by the others; and

IV. Urgent repairs to the common property or facilities ***are when the damage*** endangers the security of the titleholders ***or*** the integrity of the buildings, or prevents the proper operation of the common services. ***These repairs*** must be carried out by the Administrator in a timely fashion.

de no hacerlo o a falta de administrador, se mandarán realizar por cualquier condómino, sin necesidad de autorización previa, a quien le serán reembolsados los gastos de las mismas, repartiendo el costo entre los condóminos, debiéndose someter finalmente dicho pago a justificación y comprobación en la próxima asamblea de condóminos.

Artículo 1010. Cada condómino podrá realizar las obras y adaptaciones que correspondan a su unidad privativa, pero no podrá realizarse ninguna innovación o modificación que afecte la estructura, la cimentación, las paredes maestras, las azoteas, las redes de descargas de agua residuales, ni aquellas que puedan perjudicar la estética, la seguridad, la durabilidad o la comodidad del edificio.

Todos los proyectos de adaptación deberán aprobarse previamente por el consejo de administración del condominio.

Artículo 1010 bis.- Los condóminos y en general los ocupantes del condominio no podrán, sino con el consentimiento de la asamblea y con arreglo a las leyes aplicables:

I. Realizar acto alguno que afecte la tranquilidad y comodidad de los demás condóminos y ocupantes, o que comprometa la estabilidad, seguridad o salubridad del condominio, ni incurrir en omisiones que produzcan los mismos resultados;

If the Administrator ***fails to do so* [carry out the urgent repairs in a timely fashion]**, any titleholder can have ***the work*** done, without the need for prior authorisation, and must be reimbursed for the cost ***of the work*** after submitting the payment for justification and verification at the next Assembly. The cost ***of these repairs*** must be distributed amongst the titleholders.

Article 1010.- Each titleholder can carry out work and modifications within their private unit. However they cannot make any change or modification that affects the structure, the foundations, the supporting walls, terrace roofs, the residual water drainage system, or that might damage the building's aesthetics, security, durability, or comfort.

All modification projects **[renovations or reconstructions]** must have prior approval by the condominium's Administrative Council.

Article 1010a.- The titleholders and, in general, the occupants of the condominium, cannot do ***any of the following*** without the consent of the Assembly, and pursuant to the applicable laws:

I. Carry out any act that affects the tranquillity and comfort of the other titleholders and occupants, or that compromises the stability, security, or health of the condominium, nor any act of omission that would produce the same results;

II. Efectuar actos en el exterior o en el interior de su unidad privativa, que impida o haga ineficaz la operación de los servicios comunes e instalaciones generales, limite o dificulte el uso de las áreas comunes o ponga en riesgo la seguridad o tranquilidad de los condóminos u ocupantes;

III. Realizar obras o reparaciones en horarios nocturnos, salvo por causa de fuerza mayor;

IV. Derribar o trasplantar árboles y cambiar el uso o naturaleza de las áreas verdes;

V. Modificar, alterar ni destruir las áreas de uso común; y

VI. Poseer animales que por su número, tamaño o naturaleza afecten las condiciones de seguridad, comodidad o salubridad de los condóminos.

El infractor de estas disposiciones, independiente de las sanciones que establece este título, será responsable por el pago de los daños y perjuicios.

II. Carry out acts outside or inside their private unit that prevent or render ineffective the operation of the common services or general facilities, or that limit or impede the use of the common areas, or that put at risk the security or tranquillity of the titleholders or occupants;

III. Carry out work or repairs at night, except in case of an emergency;

IV. Cut down or transplant trees, or change the use or nature of the green areas;

V. Modify, alter, or destroy the common areas; and

VI. Possess animals that, by their number, size, or nature, affect the security, comfort, or health of the *other* titleholders.

Violators of these provisions, notwithstanding any other sanctions provided for in this Title **[of the Civil Code]**, are responsible for payment of damages and losses **[resulting from the act that contributed to their violation]**.

CAPÍTULO II – De la administración

Artículo 1011. Los bienes afectos al régimen de condominio serán administrados por quien se designe en la asamblea de condóminos, pudiendo recaer este cargo a una persona física o jurídica.

Si el cargo de administrador recae en condómino deberá acreditar previamente tener cubiertas sus cuotas.

La designación del primer administrador, cuyo encargo no podrá exceder del término de un año, compete a quien constituye el régimen de condominio.

En los condominios compuestos, la designación del administrador en caso de requerirlo, será hecha por mayoría porcentual que representen los diversos desarrollos condominales, los que expresarán su voluntad por conducto de sus administradores particulares.

En los condominios de servicios municipales, cuando no se haga la designación por los condóminos o el designado no se presentare a desempeñar su cargo, o lo abandonare, a petición de condóminos que representen el veinte por ciento de derechos, podrá la autoridad municipal hacer la designación que corresponda y estará en funciones todo el tiempo que sea necesario para ello a discreción del síndico del ayuntamiento.

En los condominios de servicios municipales destinados a cementerios, la designación siempre será hecha por el ayuntamiento del lugar de ubicación del condominio.

CHAPTER II – The Administration [actually the Administrator]

Article 1011.- The property ***incorporated into*** the condominium regime must be administered by whoever is designated by the Assembly. ***This office*** can be held by an ***individual* [physical person]** or a ***legal entity* [such as a company or an A.C.]**.

If the office of Administrator is held by a titleholder, then they must be current in payment of their condominium fees.

The appointment of the first Administrator, whose office cannot exceed a term of one year, is the responsibility of the person who establishes the condominium regime.

In compound condominiums, the appointment of a ***General*** Administrator, if required, must be made by a majority percentage of the various condominium developments ***making up the compound condominium***. Their wishes must be expressed by means of ***each of*** their individual Administrators.

In the case of Municipal Services condominiums, when the titleholders have not appointed an ***Administrator***, or the appointed ***Administrator*** does not take office or abandons it, at the request of titleholders representing twenty percent **[20%]** of the rights ***of the condominium***, the municipal authority will make the appointment, and ***the person appointed*** will be in office for as long as necessary, at the discretion of the City Manager.

In Municipal Services condominiums used as cemeteries, the appointment ***of the Administrator*** will always be made by the municipal government of the place where the condominium is located.

Cuando la asamblea de condóminos decida contratar servicios profesionales para su administración, el comité de vigilancia deberá celebrar contrato correspondiente conforme a las disposiciones aplicables, el cual no podrá exceder de un año, pudiendo ser renovado en tanto la asamblea de condóminos no determine lo contrario.

Artículo 1012. El administrador del condominio tiene las facultades y obligaciones siguientes:

I. Ser el ejecutor de los acuerdos de las asambleas de condóminos y del consejo de administración, así como el representante legal frente a terceros del condominio, con las facultades de un apoderado general judicial y para actos de administración, sin que las facultades de mandatario puedan ser sustituidas o delegadas salvo que así lo autorice expresamente el consejo de administración.

Cuando el condominio forme parte de un condominio compuesto, acatar las resoluciones que dé el administrador general de éste; en caso de conflicto por instrucciones encontradas entre el administrador del condominio compuesto y el consejo de administración, se deberán someter obligatoriamente las diferencias a arbitraje de la Procuraduría de Desarrollo Urbano, quien a la brevedad resolverá lo conducente y sin que quepa algún recurso contra tal determinación;

II. Verificar y atender la operatividad, mantenimiento de instalaciones, servicios generales y conservación de la edificación;

III. Efectuar los gastos de mantenimiento y administración;

When the Assembly decides to contract professional services for its administration, the **Administrative Council** must execute the corresponding contract in accordance with the applicable resolutions **[of the assembly]**. *The term of this contract* cannot exceed one year, and can only be renewed if the Assembly *does not object*.

Article 1012.- The Administrator of the condominium has the following authority and obligations:

I. To carry out the decisions of the Assemblies and of the Administrative Council, as well as being the legal representative of the condominium before third parties, with the power of a general legal representative, and for acts of administration. *The Administrator's* representative powers cannot be substituted or delegated unless specifically authorised by the Administrative Council.

When the condominium is part of a compound condominium, *it must* follow the decisions given by the General Administrator; in the case of a conflict of instructions between the Administrator of the compound condominium and the Administrative Council, the dispute must be submitted for arbitration to the *"Procuraduría de Desarrollo Urbano"* (Office of the Attorney General for Urban Development), which will promptly resolve the *dispute* without *the possibility of* an appeal against its decision;

II. To check and look after the operations, repair of facilities, general services, and maintenance of the buildings;

III. To make payments for maintenance and administration expenses;

IV. Cobrar las cuotas y extender los recibos que amparen los pagos a cargo de los condóminos;

V. Llevar los libros y documentación que soporten los gastos efectuados, los que deberán tener una actualización no mayor de quince días hábiles;

VI. Llevar los libros del condominio, que cuando menos deberán ser tres:

a) El primer libro, que será para asentar las actas de asambleas de condóminos;

b) El segundo libro, para asentar las actas de asamblea del consejo de administración;

c) El tercer libro, para registrar los ingresos y egresos del condominio; y

d) Cuando así lo estime necesario la asamblea de condóminos podrán llevarse los libros de registros auxiliares que se requieran; también podrán utilizarse para llevar los registros auxiliares sistemas de cómputo.

Los libros antes indicados deberán ser autorizados en la primera hoja útil por el secretario del ayuntamiento de correspondiente a la ubicación del condominio.

Al realizarse los asientos en los libros señalados se deberán conservar como apéndice de dichas actas los documentos relativos a las mismas.

IV. To collect the condominium fees, and issue receipts for payments **received** from the titleholders;

V. To keep the books and documentation that support the expenses incurred; these books must be updated no later than fifteen working days **after the expense was incurred**;

VI. To keep the condominium books, of which there must be at least three:

a) The first book is for recording the minutes of the Assemblies;

b) The second book, to record the minutes of the Administrative Council meetings;

c) The third book, to record the income and expenses of the condominium; and

d) When it is considered necessary by the Assembly, any auxiliary record books that are required; a computer system can also be used for these auxiliary records.

The aforementioned books must be authorised **[signed and stamped]** on the first usable page by the *secretario del ayuntamiento* (City Clerk) where the condominium is located.

When making entries in the indicated books, all documents related to the minutes **of the meetings** must be kept as attachments to the minutes.

Cuando por cualquier circunstancia no fuere posible asentar el acta en el libro que corresponda, para su validez, deberá ser protocolizada por notario, con residencia o jurisdicción en el municipio en que esté asentado el condominio;

When, due to any circumstance, it is not possible to enter the minutes *of a meeting* in the corresponding book, for *these minutes* to be valid, they must be protocolised by a *notario* (civil law notary) having residence or jurisdiction in the municipality where the condominium is located;

VII. Entregar en la primera quincena de los meses de abril, julio, octubre y enero de cada año, al condómino que lo solicite o tenerlo a disposición de los mismos en las oficinas de la administración, un estado de cuentas que señale:

VII. To give, within the first fifteen days of the months of April, July, October, and January of each year, to a titleholder who asks for it, or to have it available for *all titleholders* in the administration offices, a statement of accounts which shows:

a) Un informe analítico de los gastos del trimestre;

a) A written report analysing the quarter's expenses;

b) Un informe consolidado que demuestre y refleje los ingresos y las cuotas vencidas pendientes de pago;

b) A consolidated report that shows and reflects the income and overdue fees that are pending for payment;

c) Un listado general de los deudores explicando el origen de su adeudo;

c) A general list of debtors **[people who owe money to the condo]**, explaining the origin of the debt **[includes overdue fees]**;

d) Una relación de los acreedores explicando el origen de sus créditos; y

d) An accounting of creditors **[people to whom the condo owes money]**, explaining the origin of the credits; and

e) Los saldos en efectivo que existan.

e) The existing cash balance **[cash in the bank account, investments, and reserves]**.

VIII. Convocar a asamblea de condóminos;

VIII. To call an Assembly;

IX. Auxiliar y en su caso hacer que se auxilie a los comités específicos que llegaren a formarse para la realización de una obra concreta o para el logro de un fin determinado; y

IX. To directly or indirectly help special committees formed to accomplish specific work or to carry out a particular task; and

X. Las demás que le confiera este código o cualquier otro ordenamiento que le sea aplicable, la escritura constitutiva y el reglamento que se expida.

Artículo 1013. El acta que se levante con motivo de la designación del administrador y en su caso el otorgamiento de la fianza que se constituya para el desempeño de su cargo, serán protocolizadas y se tomará nota de ellas en la inscripción que al efecto se lleve en el Registro Público de la Propiedad, relativa a la constitución del régimen de propiedad en condominio.

Cuando la designación sea hecha por el ayuntamiento, bastará para su inscripción una copia certificada que expida el secretario del mismo, para proceder en los términos antes señalados.

Artículo 1013 bis.- Cuando la asamblea de condóminos designe una nueva administración, la saliente deberá entrega en un término que no exceda de quince días naturales al día de la designación, todos los documentos incluyendo los estados de cuenta, valores, muebles, inmuebles, y demás bienes que tuviera bajo su resguardo y responsabilidad, sin que dicho plazo pueda ampliarse sino por causa justificada que acrediten tal demora.

X. Any other **authority and obligations** that are conferred by this Code or any other applicable statutes, the registered establishing document, and **any** by-laws that are issued **[the condo's by-laws]. [These cannot conflict with, or override, the provisions of this Code].**

Article 1013.- The minutes of the meeting in which the Administrator was appointed, and, if required, the bond provided to guarantee the carrying out of their duties, must be protocolised and recorded in the *"Registro Público de la Propiedad"* (Public Registry of Property) corresponding to the establishment of the condominium regime.

When the appointment *of the Administrator* is made by the municipal government, a certified copy issued by its secretary **[City Clerk]** is sufficient for the purposes indicated above.

Article 1013a.- When the Assembly appoints a new administration, the outgoing **Administrator** must give **to the new Administrator**, within a term not exceeding fifteen calendar days from the day of the appointment, all documents, including the statements of account, monetary assets, furniture, buildings, and the rest of the assets under their care and responsibility; this **aforementioned term [15 calendar days]** cannot be extended without a justifiable reason to authorise such a delay.

CAPÍTULO III – Del consejo de administración

Artículo 1014. El consejo de administración se integrará con el número de miembros que se señalen en el reglamento.

Artículo 1015. Para ser consejero se requiere ser condómino u ocupante de alguna propiedad del condominio con el consentimiento del condómino y estar al corriente en el pago de cuotas al condominio.

Artículo 1016. El cargo de consejero es indelegable y honorario; sin embargo la asamblea general de condóminos, cuando así lo estime necesario podrá determinar el pago de alguna remuneración a sus integrantes, o a parte de ellos.

Artículo 1017. El consejo de administración tendrá las siguientes facultades y obligaciones:

I. Tener la representación permanente de los condóminos, para asuntos de interés común, con las facultades de un apoderado general judicial y para actos de administración;

II. Vigilar que el administrador cumpla con las obligaciones que se le imponen y pedir a éste informes y cuentas de sus gestiones, cuando lo estime necesario;

III. Reunirse cuando menos una vez al mes para recibir noticia del administrador, que podrá expresarse en forma oral u escrita respecto de la marcha y negocios del condominio verificando los estados contables y sus asientos en los libros;

CHAPTER III – The Administrative Council [Board]

Article 1014.- The Administrative Council must be made up of the number of members that are indicated in the condominium's by-laws.

Article 1015.- To be a councillor, one must be a titleholder, or an occupant of condominium property with the consent of the titleholder, and be current in the payment of condominium fees.

Article 1016.- The position of councillor is unpaid, and cannot be delegated; however, the Assembly, when it considers it necessary, can determine the payment of any remuneration **[wage or salary]** to all or some **councillors [members of the Administrative Council]**.

Article 1017. The Administrative Council has the following authority and obligations:

I. To continually represent the titleholders for matters of common interest, with the powers of a general legal representative and for acts of administration;

II. To ensure that the Administrator complies with the obligations imposed upon them, and to request from **the Administrator,** administrative reports and accounts when **the Council** deems it necessary;

III. To meet at least once a month to receive a report from the Administrator, in oral or written form, regarding the progress and business of the condominium, **and** verifying the state of the accounts and their entry into the books;

IV. Comprobar las inversiones de los fondos de mantenimiento, administración y de reserva;

V. Coadyuvar con la administración en la observancia por los condóminos del cumplimiento de sus obligaciones;

VI. Rendir a la asamblea de condóminos, anualmente durante el primer trimestre, un informe de labores así como del estado general que guardan los asuntos del condominio y su posición financiera;

VII. Cuando se trate de condominios habitacionales y comerciales, autorizar la celebración de cualquier contrato que implique la ocupación y uso de los bienes y servicios comunes, por terceros extraños a los condóminos; en este caso, los contratos que se celebren en contravención a los reglamentos y a lo aquí estipulado, serán nulos de pleno derecho;

VIII. Autorizar al administrador para otorgar o conferir directamente poder general con facultades judiciales de administración en favor de quienes estime pertinente para defensa y representación de los intereses específicos del condominio. También podrá otorgar poderes especiales; y

IV. To check the investment of the funds for maintenance, administration, and the reserves;

V. Work together with the *Administrator under* observance by the titleholders of the fulfilment of the *Administrator's and Council's* obligations;

VI. Be responsible for providing to the Assembly, annually during the first quarter, a report of *the Administrator's* work, as well as the general state of the condominium business and its financial position;

VII. When a condominium is *both* residential and commercial, to authorise the execution of any contract that involves the occupation and use of the common property and services by third parties **[lessees]**; in this case, contracts executed in violation of the by-laws and *this Code*, will be *rendered null and void*;

VIII. To authorise the Administrator to grant or directly confer a general power of attorney with legal authority of administration in favour of those considered pertinent to the defence and representation of the specific interests of the condominium **[in a lawsuit]**. *The Administrative Council* can also grant special powers of attorney **[refer to "*Part 8 Powers of Attorney & Proxies*"]**; and

IX. Los poderes que se confieran comprenden las facultades de articular y absolver posiciones, formular denuncias penales y coadyuvar con el ministerio público; adquirir bienes en remate o fuera de él haciendo las posturas y pujas que procedan celebrar los convenios de transacción, intentar y desistirse de juicios constitucionales de garantías.

En los poderes bastará y será necesario que se relacionen los siguientes puntos:

a) El instrumento mediante el cual constituyó el régimen de condominio respecto de la edificación, destacándose el lugar y fecha, el notario autorizante, el número del instrumento, los bienes genéricos que se afectaron, su ubicación y los datos de su inscripción en el Registro Público de la Propiedad;

b) Las facultades que según el reglamento de condominio tengan los consejeros, independientemente de las establecidas en la ley;

c) Las reformas que en su caso se hubieren efectuado;

IX. **These** powers of attorney that are granted **[by the Administrator or Council]** include the authority to declare and to discharge **legal** positions, to draw up criminal complaints, and to cooperate with the "*Ministerio Público*" (Public Attorney's Office); to acquire property **at auction** or outside of auction by making offers and bids, and proceeding to execute the **resulting** contracts, and to enter into and relinquish a claim for trials of constitutional guarantees **[a *juicio de amparo* (amparo suit) – unique to México, this is a suit to stop the actions of a public authority while an appeal against these authorities on constitutional grounds is undertaken – like an injunction]**.

In these **power of attorney documents**, it is sufficient and necessary to include the following points:

a) The legal instrument by which the condominium regime was established **[the *escritura constitutiva*]** in relation to the construction, indicating the place and date, the authorising *notario* (civil law notary), the **registration** number of this legal instrument, the generic property that is affected, its location, and the data concerning its registration in the "*Registro Público de la Propiedad*" (Public Registry of Property);

b) The abilities that, according to the by-laws of the condominium, have been given to the Councillors, independent of that established in the Law;

c) Any amendments that have been made **[to the *escritura constitutiva* or to the by-laws]**;

d) El acta mediante la cual se hizo la designación de los consejeros;

e) Los datos de la inscripción en el Registro Público de la Propiedad, en el cual se hubieren inscrito los instrumentos a que se refieren los puntos que anteceden; y

f) El acta de consejo en la que se acordó el otorgamiento del poder; ésta deberá ser transcrita en lo conducente.

Artículo 1018. El acta que se levante con motivo de la designación de los consejeros y sus anexos, deberá ser protocolizada por notario con residencia o jurisdicción en el municipio en que esté asentado el condominio y contener cuando menos:

I. El instrumento en el donde conste el acto mediante el cual se afectó la edificación al régimen de condominio, mencionándose el lugar y fecha, el notario autorizante, el número del instrumento, los bienes genéricos que se afectaron, su ubicación y los datos de su inscripción en el Registro Público de la Propiedad;

II. Las facultades que según el reglamento del condominio tengan los consejeros, independientemente de las establecidas en la ley;

III. Las reformas que en su caso se hubieren efectuado; y

IV. Se transcribirá en lo conducente el acta levantada.

d) The minutes *of the Assembly* at which the Councillors were appointed;

e) Data concerning the registration in the *"Registro Público de la Propiedad"* (Public Registry of Property) of **all** the documents referred to above; and

f) Pertinent parts of the minutes of the Council meeting in which it was agreed to grant the power of attorney, must be transcribed into **the document**.

Article 1018.- The minutes *of the Assembly* at which the councillors were appointed, along with its attachments, must be protocolised by a *notario* having residence or jurisdiction in the municipality in which the condominium is located, and must contain, at a minimum:

I. The legal instrument by which the condominium regime was established **[the *escritura constitutiva*]**, indicating the place and date, the authorising *notario* (civil law notary), the **registration** number of this legal instrument, the generic property that is affected, its location, and the data concerning its registration in the *"Registro Público de la Propiedad"* (Public Registry of Property);

II. The abilities that, according to the by-laws of the condominium, have been given to the Councillors, independent of those established in the Law;

III. Any amendments that have been made **[to the *escritura constitutiva* or to the by-laws]**; and

IV. A transcription of the pertinent parts of the minutes that were taken.

De la escritura que contenga la protocolización, se tomará nota en la inscripción del condominio que se lleve en el Registro Público de la Propiedad.

The legal document that contains the protocolisation must be noted in the registration of the condominium that is kept in the *"Registro Público de la Propiedad"* (Public Registry of Property).

El acta que se levante también deberá asentarse en el libro de actas del propio condominio.

These minutes must also be recorded in the condominium's minute book **[the first of three books legally required to be kept by the condo administration]**.

CAPÍTULO IV – De las asambleas

Artículo 1019. La asamblea de condóminos es el órgano supremo de la administración.

Las asambleas para los condominios compuestos y simples serán ordinarias y extraordinarias.

Artículo 1020. La asamblea ordinaria se reunirá cuando menos una vez al año, dentro del primer trimestre y en ella se tratarán los asuntos siguientes:

I. El informe general sobre el condominio, tanto en bienes y servicios como su posición financiera;

II. La elección de los integrantes del consejo de administración y en su caso, de las comisiones especiales;

III. La designación del administrador; y

IV. La aprobación del presupuesto de ingresos y de egresos para el siguiente año.

Artículo 1021. La asamblea extraordinaria se reunirá en cualquier tiempo, cuando se requiera su decisión en alguno de los casos siguientes;

I. Modificar el reglamento del condominio;

II. Realizar obras voluntarias o de mejoramiento;

III. Transformar y disponer de los bienes comunes;

CHAPTER IV – The Assemblies

Article 1019.- The Assembly of Titleholders is the supreme administrative body **[of the condominium]**.

Assemblies for compound and simple condominiums can be Ordinary and Extraordinary.

Article 1020.- The Ordinary Assembly must meet at least once a year, within the first quarter **[January, February, or March]**, and the following subjects must be dealt with in this meeting:

I. The general report on the condominium, to be as much about property and services as the condominium's financial position;

II. The election of the members of the Administrative Council and, as the case may be, of any special committees;

III. The appointment of the Administrator; and

IV. The approval of the income and expense budget for the following year.

Article 1021.- The Extraordinary Assembly can meet at any time when a decision on any of the following issues is required:

I. Modification of the condominium's by-laws;

II. Carrying out works of a voluntary nature **[not a required repair or maintenance item]** or improvements;

III. Transformation **[change from one kind of property to another]** and disposal of the common property;

IV. Acordar sobre la extinción del régimen de propiedad en condominio;

V. Incorporar nuevas áreas al régimen de propiedad en condominio o separar áreas afectas al mismo;

VI. Pedir al juez se obligue a un condómino a la venta de sus derechos;

VII. Acordar la reconstrucción del inmueble afecto al régimen de condominio; y

VIII. Las demás decisiones que correspondan a los condóminos reunidos en asamblea.

Artículo 1022. Las asambleas serán convocadas por:

I. El administrador;

II. El consejo de administración;

III. El juez de primera instancia del ramo civil con jurisdicción en el municipio de ubicación del condominio, a requerimiento de un grupo de condóminos que representen por lo menos una quinta parte de derechos; o a petición de cualquier condómino, cuando se dejen de celebrar por mas de un año; y

IV. En los casos de condominios de servicios municipales, por el presidente del municipio de ubicación del condominio.

IV. To decide on the termination of the condominium regime;

V. To incorporate new areas into the condominium regime, or to remove other areas from it;

VI. To ask a judge to force a titleholder to sell their condominium rights **[sell the unit at public auction]**;

VII. To decide on the reconstruction of the buildings belonging to the condominium regime **[after a disaster]**; and

VIII. Any other decisions that concern the titleholders meeting in an Assembly.

Article 1022.- The Assemblies must be called by:

I. The Administrator;

II. The Administrative Council;

III. A Judge of the First Instance of the civil branch having jurisdiction in the municipality where the condominium is located, at the request of a group of titleholders who represent at least one fifth **[20%]** of the condominium rights; or at the request of any titleholder, when an assembly has not been held for over one year; and

IV. In the case of Municipal Services condominiums, by the mayor of the municipality in which the condominium is located.

Artículo 1023. Para que se declare legalmente instalada la asamblea ordinaria en primera convocatoria, será necesario que concurran a ella condóminos que representen cuando menos el cincuenta y uno por ciento sobre los derechos del condominio.

Si no se reuniere el porcentaje antes señalado, se convocará por segunda vez a los condóminos para que celebren asamblea en un plazo no menor de siete, ni mayor de quince días y esta se efectuará con los que asistan.

Las resoluciones que se tomen en las asambleas ordinarias serán válidas cuando se decida el negocio por condóminos que tengan la mayoría porcentual de los derechos sobre el condominio, que estén representados por los asistentes a la misma.

Por lo que se refiere a la asamblea extraordinaria, podrá celebrarse con el número de condóminos que asistan, pero sólo serán válidos los acuerdos que en ella se tomen, si son aprobados por condóminos que representen cuando menos el setenta y cinco por ciento de los derechos sobre el condominio. Esta aprobación se tendrá, ya sea mediante asamblea en la que concurran condóminos cuyos votos representen tal porcentaje, o se complementen en los siguientes treinta días naturales a su celebración, con condóminos ausentes a la asamblea, quienes en forma auténtica se manifiesten sabedores de los acuerdos tomados y los aprueben.

Los acuerdos tomados en asamblea legalmente constituida, obligan a los ausentes, disidentes y en su caso, a los ocupantes por cualquier título.

Article 1023.- For an Ordinary Assembly to be legally convened on its first call, it is necessary that titleholders representing at least fifty-one percent **[51%]** of the condominium rights participate **[in person or by proxy. Refer to *"Part 8 Powers of Attorney & Proxies"*]**.

If the percentage indicated above is not met, a second call to the titleholders must be made for a *new* Assembly, to be held in no less than seven **[7]** and no more than fifteen **[15]** days, and this *new* Assembly can take place with any number *of titleholders* who attend.

Resolutions taken in Ordinary Assemblies are valid when the matter is agreed upon by titleholders that have the majority percentage of the condominium rights that are represented by the attendees of the *assembly*.

As for the Extraordinary Assembly, it can be held with any number of titleholders who attend, but the agreements made will only be valid if they are approved by titleholders who represent at least seventy-five percent **[75%]** of the total condominium rights. This approval must *be made* either by means of *an* Assembly in which titleholders participate, and whose votes represent such a percentage **[75%]**, or *by votes* provided in the following thirty calendar days *after the assembly* by the absent titleholders, who explicitly declare themselves to be genuinely knowledgeable of the agreements, and approve them.

Agreements made in a legally established Assembly are binding upon the absentees, those who disagreed, and, as the case may be, on the occupants *of the condominium* by any title.

Quien no haya asistido a la celebración de la asamblea alegando no haber sido convocado en forma legal, podrá demandar la inoponibilidad de los acuerdos tomados en la misma, dentro de los siguientes treinta días naturales a la fecha de su celebración, siempre y cuando no hayan ejecutado actos que impliquen la aprobación de los acuerdos a que se oponen, o su realización fuera hecha con la advertencia de que no implica conformidad con la misma. La resolución judicial que se dicte sólo tendrá efectos respecto de quien la promovió.

Artículo 1024. Las reglas anteriormente señaladas rigen para los condominios compuestos y para los condominios simples.

Las asambleas serán presididas por quien designen los condóminos asistentes a ellas, tomándose la votación por mayoría de personas asistentes a la misma, independientemente del porcentaje que representen en el condominio. El administrador podrá ser designado presidente de la asamblea.

Artículo 1025. Las convocatorias para la celebración de la asamblea serán suscritas por quien las haga.

Las asambleas deberán verificarse invariablemente en el municipio de la ubicación del condominio, buscando siempre la mayor comodidad y fácil acceso a los condóminos; preferentemente se deberán desarrollar en la unidad condominal.

La convocatoria para asamblea ordinaria deberá hacerse cuando menos con quince días naturales de anticipación a la fecha en que deba celebrarse.

Anyone who did not attend an Assembly, alleging that they were not legally notified, can, within thirty calendar days following the date of the **assembly**, demand the inadmissibility of the agreements reached in the **assembly**, as long as they have not taken actions that imply approval of the agreements that they oppose, or if these actions were taken after making it known that **these actions** do not imply approval. **Any** judicial decision that is issued, will only affect the person who initiated **the claim**.

Article 1024.- The previous rules **[Articles 1019 through 1023]** apply to compound and to simple condominiums.

Assemblies must be presided over **[chaired]** by whoever the attending titleholders designate, by taking a majority vote of **the** persons attending **the Assembly**, independent of the percentage which they represent in the condominium **[a non-proportional vote]**. The Administrator can be designated Chair of the Assembly.

Article 1025.- The call for the Assembly must be signed by the person making it.

Assemblies must always take place in the municipality where the condominium is located, in a place that provides the greatest comfort and ease of access for the titleholders; preferably in the condominium unit.

The call for an Ordinary Assembly must be made at least fifteen **[15]** calendar days before the anticipated date of the **Assembly**.

La convocatoria para asamblea extraordinaria deberá hacerse cuando menos con veinte días naturales de anticipación a la fecha en que deba celebrarse.

En ambos casos, la convocatoria se fijará en los lugares visibles de la edificación del condominio en la fecha en que se expida. Además, deberá citarse por medio del servicio postal con acuse de recibo, a los condóminos que lo requieran en el domicilio que para estos casos tengan registrado en la administración. El depósito de la correspondencia en el correo, deberá hacerse con la misma anticipación que se señala para su fijación, debiéndose conservar los acuses de recibo para acreditar lo anterior.

Cuando la convocatoria se formule por la autoridad judicial o la municipal, bastará que se publique con la misma anticipación en uno de los periódicos de amplia circulación en el Estado, así como en el Periódico Oficial "El Estado de Jalisco" y sin perjuicio de que se coloque un ejemplar de la convocatoria en los lugares visibles del condominio.

La convocatoria deberá señalar el día y la hora para la cual se cita a la asamblea, la clase de asamblea a verificar, el lugar de la reunión y los puntos a considerarse.

Cualquier asunto tratado en la asamblea y que no éste comprendido en el orden del día, no tendrá fuerza legal alguna, salvo el caso de que hayan estado representados el cien por ciento de personas e intereses.

The call for an Extraordinary Assembly must be made at least twenty **[20]** calendar days before the anticipated date of the *Assembly*.

In both cases, the call notice must be posted in a visible place in the condominium buildings on the date of its issuance. In addition, titleholders who demand it, must be notified by registered mail sent to the address registered with the administration. Mailing of correspondence must *allow for* the same advance notice as that required for *calling the Assembly*. Delivery receipts must be kept as proof *of this advance warning*.

When the call notice *for an Assembly* is issued by a judicial or municipal authority, it is sufficient that it be published with the same advance notice in a newspaper with broad circulation in the State, as well as in the Official Newspaper *"El Estado de Jalisco"*, and, notwithstanding this, the call notice must also be posted in visible places within the condominium unit.

The call notice must show the date and time of the Assembly, confirm the type of Assembly **[Ordinary or Extraordinary]**, the place the *Assembly* will be held, and the items for consideration **[the Order of the Day]**.

Any matter dealt with in the Assembly, which is not included in the Order of the Day, will not have any legal force, except in the case where one hundred percent **[100%]** of the titleholders and interests **[condo rights]** are represented *at the Assembly*.

CAPÍTULO V – De las cuotas

Artículo 1026. Los condóminos deberán contribuir para sufragar los gastos de mantenimiento y operación de las instalaciones y servicios del condominio, como también para constituir y conservar fondos de reserva, en base al porcentaje que sobre el condominio represente cada unidad privativa; pero cuando un condominio conste de diferentes elementos y comprenda varias escaleras, patios, jardines, obras e instalaciones como ascensores, montacargas, antenas y otros elementos o aparatos, de uso exclusivo de uno o varios condóminos, los gastos que por ello se originen serán a cargo de quienes directa y exclusivamente se sirvan.

Cuando se decrete la realización de una obra de mejoramiento o voluntaria, en el mismo acuerdo deberán fijarse las bases para cubrir su costo.

Tratándose de condominios de servicios municipales y cuando no hubiere acuerdo entre los condóminos, la fijación de las cuotas condominales deberá hacerse por el tesorero del municipio de la ubicación del condominio.

Artículo 1027. Cuando se trate de condominios compuestos se seguirán las mismas reglas para el pago de las cuotas, tanto ordinarias como extraordinarias en que se incurran.

CHAPTER V – Fees

Article 1026.- The titleholders must contribute to defray the expenses for the maintenance and operation of the facilities and services of the condominium, and also to create and maintain reserve funds, on the basis of the percentage of the condominium **rights** represented by each private unit; but, when a condominium consists of different elements and contains several stairs, patios, gardens, works and facilities such as elevators, freight elevators, antennas and other components or equipment **that are** for the exclusive use of one or more titleholders **[not available for use by all owners, and, therefore, not common property]**, the expenses arising **from these components or equipment** must be paid by those who directly and exclusively benefit **from them**.

When it is directed **[by an Assembly]** to carry out improvements or voluntary work, the basis for covering these costs must be established in the same agreement **[of the Assembly]**.

In Municipal Services condominiums, when there is no agreement among the titleholders, setting of the condominium fees will be made by the treasurer of the municipality where the condominium is located.

Article 1027.- When **it involves a** Compound condominium, **the condominium** must follow these same rules for payment of the fees **whether** they are incurred as Ordinary **[budgeted fees approved at an assembly]** or Extraordinary **[approved improvements or emergency requirements]** **fees**.

Artículo 1028. Las cuotas a cargo de los condóminos deberán pagarse por adelantado, precisamente en la fecha establecida y, en caso de no hacerse, se pagará como perjuicio hasta la cantidad que resulte de considerar el tipo de interés moratorio promedio que se fije por las dos mayores instituciones de crédito en el país, en préstamos ordinarios quirografarios a treinta días, según se determine en el reglamento.

Artículo 1029. Es título ejecutivo el estado de cuenta que se emita después de haber transcurrido noventa días de haberse vencido el plazo para el pago y que sea suscrito por el administrador con la aprobación del presidente del consejo de administración.

El estado de cuenta aquí indicado deberá precisar con toda claridad el importe y origen del adeudo, ya que éstos pueden provenir tanto por falta de pago de cuotas, como por alguna otra responsabilidad que se derive a cargo del condómino, asimismo el pago de los perjuicios que causen.

Cuando se trate de condominios de servicios municipales el cobro de los adeudos podrá hacerse por conducto de la Tesorería Municipal del lugar de ubicación del condominio, considerándose para todos los efectos legales como créditos municipales.

Article 1028.- The fees payable by the titleholders must be paid in advance, precisely on the established date. In the event a payment is not made, ***the delinquent titleholder*** must pay as a penalty up to the amount that results from calculating the average penalty interest rate set by the two largest lending institutions in the country, for ordinary unsecured thirty-day loans **[personal loans]**, in accordance with what is determined in the by-laws.

Article 1029.- The statement of accounts that is issued after ninety days have passed from the due date for payment **[of the fees]**, and that is signed by the Administrator with the approval of the President of the Administrative Council, is an enforceable document **[needed for any legal action – fees are not legally collectible until at least 90 days have passed]**.

This statement of accounts mentioned herein must specify clearly the amount and origin of the debts ***owed to the condominium***, since these can result from a lack of payment of fees, or any other responsibility that is derived from the charges to a titleholder **[such as interest and sanctions or expenses caused by damages]**, and also the payment of the damages that they cause.

In Municipal Services condominiums, collection of debts can be made by means of the Municipal Treasury of the place where the condominium is located, which must consider these, for all legal purposes, as municipal credits.

Los ocupantes o usuarios del condominio por cualquier título, son solidariamente responsables con los condóminos del pago de las cuotas ordinarias y extraordinarias que se establezcan, así como de cualquier responsabilidad que les resulte a sus acciones.

Artículo 1029 bis.- Todo condómino tendrá derecho a que se le expida el estado de cuenta que guarde en el condominio.

Cuando se celebre un contrato traslativo de dominio en relación a una unidad privativa, el notario público que elabore la escritura, deberá exigir a la parte vendedora la entrega de la constancia de no adeudo expedida por el administrador del condominio.

Artículo 1030. Las obligaciones a cargo del condominio, se ejecutarán sobre los fondos del patrimonio común; en caso de no ajustar con el mismo, el excedente deberá ser pagado proporcionalmente, al interés que cada condómino represente.

Occupants or users of the condominium by any title **[such as tenants or renters]**, are jointly responsible along with the titleholders for the payment of Ordinary and Extraordinary fees that are established, as well as any responsibility that results from *these occupants' or users'* actions.

Article 1029a.- Every titleholder has the right to be issued a statement of accounts kept by the condominium.

When a contract is executed to transfer *title* in relation to a private unit **[when the unit is sold]**, the *notario* (civil law notary) who prepares the public document **[transfer of title]** must ask the seller to deliver a declaration, issued by the Administrator of the condominium, *that there are no outstanding debts owed to the condominium*.

Article 1030.- The financial obligations of the condominium must be *paid* from the common capital funds. In the event that *these funds* are *not sufficient*, the excess must be paid *by the titleholders* proportionally to the interest that each titleholder represents **[their condo rights]**.

CAPITULO VI – De las controversias

Artículo 1031. Cuando surjan controversias entre los condóminos por los derechos que les competan en el uso de sus unidades privativas y bienes comunes, se resolverán conforme a las reglas siguientes:

I. Las controversias entre condóminos deberán sujetarse necesariamente al arbitraje del consejo de administración;

II. Cuando estas controversias se susciten en condominios de servicios municipales, se deberán someter al arbitraje del secretario del ayuntamiento del lugar de ubicación del condominio;

III. El Código de Procedimientos Civiles del Estado será supletorio en estos negocios; y

IV. Las demás controversias que surjan, serán ventiladas ante el juez de primera instancia del domicilio de ubicación del condominio.

Artículo 1032. El condómino que reiteradamente deje de cumplir sus obligaciones o injustificadamente cause conflictos a los demás condóminos será demandado por el administrador ante el Juez de Primera Instancia de la ubicación del condominio, para que en subasta pública se vendan al mejor postor sus derechos condominales, en los términos que para los remates señala el Código de Procedimientos Civiles del Estado.

CHAPTER VI – Disputes

Article 1031.- When a dispute occurs between titleholders over the rights concerning the use of their private units and the common property, *__this dispute__* must be settled according to the following rules:

I. Disputes between titleholders must be *__settled by__* arbitration by the Administrative Council, whose decisions must be complied with **[binding arbitration]**;

II. When these disputes occur in a Municipal Services condominium, they must be submitted for arbitration by the Secretary of the municipal government where the condominium is located;

III. The "*Código de Procedimientos Civiles del Estado*" (Code of Civil Procedures of the State) must be used as an adjunct to these proceedings; and

IV. Any other disputes that occur will be aired before a Judge of First Instance of the place where the condominium is located.

Article 1032.- A titleholder who repeatedly fails to fulfil their obligations, or unjustifiably causes conflicts with the other titleholders, can be sued by the Administrator before a Judge of First Instance of the place where the condominium is located, so that their condominium rights can be sold to the highest bidder at public auction under the terms for auction sales that are indicated in the "*Código de Procedimientos Civiles del Estado*" (Code of Civil Procedures of the State). **[This means selling the unit – condo rights are inseparable. Refer to "*Part 13 Rules for Public Property Auctions*"]**

A la demanda se acompañarán como documentos fundatorios de la misma, copia de la escritura de constitución del régimen de condominio, las reformas que hubiere sufrido la misma, certificado de gravámenes expedido por el Registro Público de la Propiedad y del testimonio de la escritura que contenga la protocolización del Acta de Asamblea Extraordinaria que acuerde la medida, misma que para ser válida deberá ser tomada por mas de la mitad del total de los condóminos. En los casos de los condominios compuestos, bastará con que lo acuerden el mas de la mitad de los titulares de la unidad condominal a la que pertenezca el condómino cuya exclusión se promueve.

El juez dará entrada a la demanda y dará vista al condómino afectado, previniéndole para que en el término de ley haga la designación del perito valuador que le corresponde apercibiéndole que de no hacerlo lo hará el juzgado en su rebeldía.

Rendido el peritaje se señalará día y hora para que tenga verificativo la almoneda.

Artículo 1033. Si quien no cumple con sus obligaciones fuese ocupante no propietario, será demandado por la desocupación del departamento, vivienda, casa o local, por el administrador, previo consentimiento del condominio. Si éste se opusiere, se procederá contra ambos, en términos del artículo anterior.

Accompanying this lawsuit must be supporting documents: a copy of the registered establishing document of the condominium regime, **any** amendments made to **this document**, a certificate of liens **[or encumbrances]** issued by the "*Registro Público de la Propiedad*" (Public Registry of Property), and a *testimonio* **[an original document created by a *notario* – a certified copy is not sufficient]** of the registered public document that contains the protocolisation of the Minutes of the Extraordinary Assembly that decided to take this measure **[proceed against the titleholder]**. For **this decision** to be valid, it must have been agreed to by more than half of all the titleholders **[non-proportional vote]**. In the case of a compound condominium, it will be sufficient that it is agreed to by more than half of the title holders of the condominium unit to which the titleholder whose exclusion is being sought belongs.

The judge will enter the suit, and will serve notice on the affected titleholder, giving them warning so that they can, in the period of time established by the law, designate an expert appraiser that suits them, advising them that if they fail to do so, they will be in default, and that the court will **appoint an expert appraiser**.

Once the expert opinion is rendered, the date and time of the public auction will be determined **[by the judge]**.

Article 1033.- If the person who does not fulfil their obligations is an occupant, rather than an owner, they can be sued to vacate the apartment, housing unit, house, or business premises by the Administrator, with the prior consent of the condominium. If **the titleholder** is opposed to **this eviction**, action can be taken against both of them under the terms of the previous article.

CAPÍTULO VII – De la destrucción y extinción

Artículo 1034. Si la edificación afecta al régimen de condominio se destruyere en su totalidad o en una proporción que represente por lo menos las tres cuartas partes de su valor, cualesquiera de los condóminos podrá pedir la división de los bienes comunes con arreglo a las disposiciones generales sobre la copropiedad.

Si la destrucción no alcanza la gravedad que se indica, mediante asamblea extraordinaria se resolverá sobre su reconstrucción.

Los condóminos que queden en minoría están obligados a contribuir a la reconstrucción en la proporción que les corresponda, o a vender sus derechos a los mayoritarios, según valuación pericial.

Las reglas anteriores se observarán también en caso de ruina o de inoperabilidad de la edificación.

CHAPTER VII – Destruction And Termination

Article 1034.- If the buildings making up the condominium regime are completely destroyed, or in a proportion that represents at least three-quarters **[75%]** of their value, any one of the titleholders can ask for the division of the common properties in accordance with the general provisions about co-ownership **[see *"Part 4 – Co-Ownership"* in this book]**.

If the destruction is not as serious as indicated *in the previous paragraph*, reconstruction must be resolved by means of an Extraordinary Assembly.

The titleholders that are in the minority **[of the vote for reconstruction at the Extraordinary Assembly]** are obligated to contribute to the reconstruction in the proportion that corresponds to them **[their condo rights]**, or to sell their rights to those in the majority according to an expert valuation. **[This actually means selling their units, since the condo rights are inseparable from the property rights.]**

The previous rules must also be observed in the case of bankruptcy *of the condominium,* or if the buildings *become unusable or condemned*.

CAPÍTULO VIII – De los condominios habitacionales duplex

Artículo 1035. Esta modalidad de condominios es aplicable exclusivamente, para aprovechar la superficie e infraestructura urbana de un predio sobre el que se edifican dos viviendas.

Artículo 1036. Cada una de las viviendas representará la mitad de la totalidad de los derechos comunes del inmueble.

Artículo 1037. Serán aplicables para el funcionamiento de este tipo de condominios las siguientes bases:

I. Deberán constituirse mediante escritura pública, en la que se insertará la descripción general del condominio; descripción particular de cada una de las viviendas, los permisos para su edificación o habitabilidad que otorguen las autoridades de urbanización; el pago de los impuestos y derechos que se generen; los planos a escala del inmueble y de cada vivienda; y en su caso, el reglamento particular del condominio;

II. Las decisiones que se tomen para el mantenimiento y conservación del condominio, así como cualquier variación al mismo, deberán siempre de tomarse por común acuerdo entre los condóminos;

III. Los gastos que se originen por la conservación del condominio serán siempre por partes iguales;

CHAPTER VIII – Residential Duplex condominiums

Article 1035.- The ***Residential Duplex condominium*** is exclusively intended to take advantage of the surface area and urban infrastructure of a property on which two housing units are built.

Article 1036.- Each one of the housing units represents half of the total of the common rights of the buildings.

Article 1037.- The following rules apply to the operation of this type of condominium:

I. It must be established by means of a publicly registered document **[an *escritura constitutiva*]** into which the general description of the condominium must be inserted; a specific description of each of the housing units; the permits for construction or occupancy which are granted by the town planning authorities; the payment of the taxes and rights that apply; to-scale construction plans of the property and each housing unit; and, if applicable, the by-laws that apply to the condominium;

II. Decisions regarding maintenance and repair of the condominium, as well as any modifications, must always be made by common agreement between the titleholders;

III. The expenses that arise for the ***maintenance and repair*** of the condominium must always ***be shared*** equally **[fifty-fifty]**;

IV. Los condóminos deberán usar en igualdad de circunstancias los bienes de uso común, pudiéndose delimitar para uso reservado de cada una de las unidades habitacionales los espacios correspondientes a las azoteas y lugares de estacionamiento;

V. En caso de destrucción, ruina o inoperabilidad de la edificación, los condóminos deberán decidir conjuntamente sobre la reconstrucción, demolición o enajenación del inmueble;

VI. En caso de que los condóminos no se pongan de acuerdo sobre los cuatro puntos anteriores, cualquiera de ellos podrá ocurrir ante la Procuraduría del Desarrollo Urbano en procedimiento arbitral forzoso, para que con audiencia del otro condómino y siguiendo las formalidades que para el trámite de los incidentes regula el Código de Procedimientos Civiles del Estado, dicte la resolución que corresponda, la cual será obligatoria para las partes involucradas. Cuando existan acreedores hipotecarios o quirografarios, también deberá dárseles intervención para salvaguarda de sus intereses; y

VII. Cada una de las unidades habitacionales podrá ser enajenada libremente por sus titulares, sin que el otro condómino tenga para ello derecho al tanto.

Artículo 1038. Cuando surja alguna circunstancia no prevista en el reglamento particular que se emita para el condominio o en éste capítulo, se aplicarán de manera supletoria las bases que para la copropiedad se refiere en este código.

IV. The common property must be used equally by the titleholders, spaces for terrace roofs and parking can be defined for the reserved use of each of the residential units;

V. In the event of the destruction, bankruptcy *of the condominium*, or non-usability of the building, the titleholders must decide jointly about the reconstruction, demolition, or sale of the real estate;

VI. In the event the titleholders do not agree on the four previous points, either one of them can appear before the *"Procuraduría del Desarrollo Urbano"* (Office of the Attorney General for Urban Development) in a binding arbitration procedure, so that *the judge* will hear the other titleholder and, following the protocols for the procedures for the circumstances regulated by the *"Código de Procedimientos Civiles del Estado"* (Code of Civil Procedures of the State), will issue a corresponding decision which will be binding on the parties involved. When a mortgage creditor or unregistered title deed exists, *the judge* must give the *holders of these* intervenor status to safeguard their interests; and

VII. Each of the residential units can be freely sold by its title holders; without the other titleholder having the right to first refusal.

Article 1038.- When an unforeseen circumstance arises in the *condominium's* by-laws or in this chapter **[of the Code]**, the rules for co-ownership related in this Code will be applied in a supplementary manner **[see *"Part 4 – Co-Ownership"* in this book]**.

PART 4 – Co-Ownership

Civil Code of the State of Jalisco
Book 3 – Title 5
Articles 961 – 1000

Relevance to Condominiums

The portion of the Civil Code that forms the condo law (see "***Part 3 – The Jalisco Condo Law***") deals with the special case of co-ownership of common property in a condo.

However, there's another section of the Code that deals with co-ownership of property in general, and defines these rights and obligations.

In a condo regime, the more specific rules (the condo law) take priority over the general rules in this section, but many of these general rules can also apply in a condo.

In a condo apartment, the walls between units could either be part of the common property of the condo (each owner would only be responsible for the exterior finish of the wall), or be co-owned by both neighbours (both would be jointly responsible for repairs and maintenance).

In a gated condominium, rules of co-ownership might also apply to walls straddling the property line between two lots, or to the perimeter wall of the condo. If a wall between two lots is entirely on one lot (the most common situation), then it is the responsibility of that owner. If it straddles the property line, it is either the responsibility of the one who built it, or, if this can't be determined, the joint responsibility of both.

There are four possibilities for the perimeter wall of your condo:

1. Straddle the property line between your condo and an adjoining property.

    Both properties are jointly responsible for maintenance and repair, unless it can be proven that one party paid for the wall (then this party owns it, and is responsible).

2. Be entirely on your condominium property.

    Your condo (all owners) is responsible for repair and maintenance if the wall is listed as part of the common property.

    If it isn't listed as common property, the owners on the perimeter of the condo are each responsible for their section of the wall.

3. Be entirely on your condo's property, but the exterior finish has been applied by the owner of the adjoining property, or a later change in width or other extension has been added by the owner of the adjoining property.

    This can happen if your wall was built when the adjoining property was undeveloped, and the surface of the wall facing into this adjoining property was unfinished.

Your condo is the exclusive owner of the main structure of the wall, and any finish or extension later applied to it by the other property owner belongs to them, and is their responsibility.

The neighbour needs the permission of your condo to finish or extend this wall on their side. They don't need your permission to build another wall right up against yours (assuming this would be on their own property).

4. Be entirely on the adjoining property, but the exterior finish on the condo side has been applied by your condo, or a later change in width or other extension has been added by your condo.

This can happen if the other wall was built when your condo property was undeveloped, and the surface of the wall facing into the condo from this adjoining property was unfinished.

The adjoining property is the exclusive owner of the main structure of the wall, and any finish or extension later applied to it by your condo belongs to the condo, and is your condo's responsibility.

Your condo would need the permission of the owner of the adjoining property to finish or extend this wall on the condo side. Your condo doesn't need permission to build your own wall right up against that of the adjoining property (assuming this would be on the condo's own property).

Versions of Laws Used

Codes and laws are living documents that are amended frequently by the level of government that issued them.

This section contains an excerpt from the *Código Civil del Estado de Jalisco* (Civil Code of the State of Jalisco), that took effect on **September 14, 1995**, and was last amended on ***December 20, 2014***.

Sections of the Laws Used

The excerpt from the **Jalisco Civil Code** translated in this section is *Libro Tercero – Título Quinto*:

Libro Tercero (Book Three) is titled "*De los bienes, su propiedad y sus diferentes manifestaciones*" (Property, Its Ownership, and Its Different Forms).

Título Quinto (Title Five) is titled "*De La Propiedad*" (Ownership).

CÓDIGO CIVIL DEL ESTADO DE JALISCO	CIVIL CODE OF THE STATE OF JALISCO

LIBRO TERCERO

BOOK THREE

TÍTULO QUINTO – DE LA PROPIEDAD

TITLE FIVE – OWNERSHIP

CAPÍTULO IV – De La Copropiedad

CHAPTER IV – Co-Ownership

Artículo 961. Hay copropiedad cuando un bien o un derecho pertenecen pro indiviso a varias personas.

Article 961.- Co-ownership exists when a property or right belongs to several people with an undivided interest **[common property – all have a joint share of the undivided whole]**.

Artículo 962. Los que por cualquier título tienen el dominio común de un bien, no pueden ser obligados a conservarlo indiviso.

Article 962.- No titleholder who has a common **right to control and use** a property, can be forced to maintain **that property as if it were** undivided **[it must be maintained jointly]**.

Artículo 963. Si el dominio no es divisible, o el bien no admite cómoda división y los partícipes no se convienen en que sea vendido o adjudicado a uno de ellos, se procederá a su venta y a la repartición de su precio entre los interesados.

Article 963.- If the **right to control and use the property** is not divisible, or if the property cannot be easily divided **[usually because of the physical make up of the property]**, and the **co-owners** cannot agree on what can be sold or assigned to one of them, **the property** must be sold, and the proceeds divided amongst the stakeholders.

Artículo 964. A falta de contrato o disposición especial, se regirá la copropiedad por las disposiciones siguientes y, en último término, por las que rigen toda sociedad de hecho.

Article 964.- In the absence of a contract or special decree, co-ownership must be governed by the following rules **[in this section of the Code]** and, as a last resort, by those **laws** that govern all general partnerships.

Artículo 965. Mientras varias personas permanezcan en la indivisión de una propiedad, cualquiera de ellas podrá exigir a las demás que se haga la designación de un administrador, el que será nombrado por mayoría de votos calculada conjuntamente por personas y por intereses. Si no hubiere mayoría, el juez hará la designación de entre los copropietarios.

Article 965.- While several people continue to have common ownership, any party can ask the others to appoint an administrator, who must be named by a majority of votes jointly calculated by persons and interests **[ownership percentages]**. If there is no majority, a judge will make the appointment from amongst the co-owners.

Artículo 966. El concurso de los partícipes, tanto en los beneficios como en las cargas, será proporcional a sus respectivas porciones.

Se presumirán iguales, mientras no se pruebe lo contrario, las porciones correspondientes a los partícipes en la comunidad.

Artículo 967. Cada partícipe podrá servirse de los bienes comunes, siempre que disponga de ellos conforme a su uso y de manera que no perjudique el interés de la comunidad, ni impida a los copropietarios aprovecharlos según su derecho.

Artículo 968. Todo copropietario tiene derecho para obligar a los partícipes a contribuir a los gastos de conservación del bien o derecho común. Sólo puede eximirse de esta obligación quien renuncie a la parte que le pertenece en el dominio.

Artículo 969. Ninguno de los condueños podrá, sin el consentimiento de los demás, hacer alteraciones en el bien común, aunque de ello pudieran resultar ventajas para todos.

Artículo 970. Para la administración del bien común, serán obligatorios todos los acuerdos de la mayoría de los copropietarios; calculada ésta conjuntamente por personas e intereses.

Artículo 971. Si no hubiere mayoría, el juez oyendo a los interesados, resolverá lo que debe hacerse dentro de lo propuesto por los mismos.

Article 966.- Co-operation amongst the *co-owners*, both for the benefits and the obligations, must be proportional to their respective portions **[percentage of ownership]**.

Until proven otherwise, the percentages *of ownership* in the *co-owned property* corresponding to each *co-owner* are presumed equal.

Article 967.- Each *co-owner* can make use of the common property, provided that they use it in accordance with its purpose and so as not to harm the interest of the community, nor to prevent the *other* co-owners from using it according to their right.

Article 968.- Each co-owner has the right to force the *other co-owners* to contribute to the costs of maintaining the property or common right. Only those who renounce the *right to control and use* the part that belongs to them can be exempted from this obligation.

Article 969.- None of the co-owners can, without the consent of the others, make alterations to the common property, even though it might be for the benefit of all.

Article 970.- For the administration of the common property, all agreements of the majority of the co-owners are binding; jointly calculated by persons and interests **[percentage of ownership]**.

Article 971.- If there is no majority, a judge hearing the stakeholders will determine what should be done, based on what they are proposing.

Artículo 972. Cuando parte del bien perteneciere exclusivamente a un copropietario o algunos de ellos, y otra fuere común, sólo a ésta será aplicable la disposición anterior.

Artículo 973. Todo condueño tiene la plena propiedad de la parte alícuota que le corresponda y la de sus frutos y utilidades, pudiendo en consecuencia enajenarla, cederla o hipotecarla y aun ser sustituido por otro en su aprovechamiento, salvo si se tratare de derecho intransmisible. Pero el efecto de la enajenación o de la hipoteca en relación a los condueños estará limitado a la porción que se le adjudique en la división al cesar la comunidad. Los condueños gozan del derecho del tanto.

Artículo 974. Los copropietarios del bien indiviso no pueden enajenar a extraños su parte alícuota respectiva, si el copartícipe quiere hacer uso del derecho del tanto. A este efecto, el copropietario notificará a los demás por medio de notario o judicialmente la enajenación que tuviere convenida, para que dentro de los ocho días siguientes hagan uso del derecho del tanto. Por el solo transcurso del término se pierde el derecho.

Cuando la venta está simplemente propalada y el copropietario ejercita el derecho del tanto, implica una venta directa del copropietario enajenante en favor del que ejercita el tanto; cuando la venta ha sido consumada los copropietarios preteridos pueden ejercitar el derecho de retracto por medio del cual el copartícipe actor se subroga en todos los derechos y obligaciones del comprador.

Article 972.- When part of the property belongs exclusively to one co-owner or **only** to some of them, and the remainder is common, the previous provision applies only to the **common property [and not the solely-owned or partially-owned property]**.

Article 973.- Each co-owner has full ownership of the pro-rated portion **of the co-owned property** that corresponds to **this owner**, as well as its values and benefits, and can, therefore, sell it, assign it, or mortgage it, and be replaced by another **owner**, except in the case of a nontransferable right. But the effect of the disposal or mortgage in relation to the **other** co-owners is limited to the portion that would be allotted to this owner upon dissolving the partnership. The co-owners have the right of first refusal.

Article 974.- Co-owners of a common property cannot sell their respective, pro-rated portion to a stranger if **another** co-owner wants to exercise their right of first refusal. To this end, the co-owner must notify the **other co-owners** by means of a *notario* (civil law notary), or other legal means, stipulating the offer of the sale, so that within the following eight [8] days they can exercise their right of first refusal. Once this term has passed [**8 days**] the right **of first refusal** is lost.

Once the sale is disclosed, and a co-owner exercises the right of first refusal, a direct sale from the selling co-owner to the one who exercised their **right** is implied. When the sale has been completed, the co-owners **who chose not to exercise their rights** can exercise the right of **retraction of the sale**, by means of which the co-owner **who exercised the right takes on** all the rights and obligations of the buyer **[will be paid back by the others – all co-owners will then jointly co-own the sold share]**.

Mientras no se haya hecho la notificación o se haya consumado el plazo, la enajenación no producirá efecto legal alguno.

Artículo 975. Si varios propietarios de bien indiviso hicieren uso del derecho del tanto, será preferido el que represente mayor parte o si fuesen iguales, entonces el más antiguo. Ante toda igualdad, el designado por la suerte; salvo pacto en contrario.

Artículo 976. Cuando haya constancia que demuestre quien costeó la pared que divide los predios, el que la hizo es dueño exclusivo de ella; pero si consta que se fabricó por los colindantes o no consta quien la edifico, es de propiedad común.

Artículo 977. Se presume la copropiedad mientras no haya signo exterior que demuestre lo contrario en:

I. Las paredes divisorias de los edificios contiguos, hasta el punto común de elevación;

II. Las paredes divisorias de los jardines o corrales, situadas en poblado o en el campo; y

III. Las cercas, vallados y setos vivos que dividan los predios rústicos. Si las construcciones no tienen una misma altura, sólo hay presunción de copropiedad hasta la altura de la construcción menos elevada.

As long as this notification has not been made, or the term **[8 days]** has not expired, a sale will have no legal effect.

Article 975.- If several owners of the common property want to exercise the right of first refusal, preference will be given to **the co-owner** who represents the largest part, or, if they are all equal, to the the one **who has been an owner the longest**. Unless otherwise agreed, if each is equal, the selection will be made by chance **[a draw or lottery]**.

Article 976.- When there is evidence that shows who paid the cost of the wall that divides **two** properties, whoever **paid these costs** is the exclusive owner of **the wall**; but if it is evident that it was built by **both** adjoining owners, or **if it** is not evident who built it, then it is common property.

Article 977.- Co-ownership is presumed in **the following** as long as there is no outward indications contrary **to co-ownership**:

I. Dividing walls of abutting buildings **[in contact with each other]**, up to the point of common height;

II. Dividing walls of gardens or animal enclosures, located in the city or the countryside; and

III. Fences, barbed wire, and hedges that divide rural properties. If these constructions do not have the same height, **then** there is only the presumption of co-ownership up to the height of the lowest construction.

Artículo 978. Hay signo contrario a la copropiedad cuando:

I. Hay ventanas o huecos abiertos en la pared divisoria de los edificios;

II. Conocidamente toda la pared, vallado, cerca o seto están construidos sobre el terreno de una de las fincas y no por mitad entre una y otra de las dos contiguas;

III. La pared soporte las cargas y carreras, pesos y armaduras de una de las posesiones y no de la contigua;

IV. La pared divisoria entre patios, jardines y otros predios, esté construida de modo que la albardilla caiga hacia una sola de las propiedades;

V. La pared divisoria construida de mampostería presente piedras llamadas pasaderas, que de distancia en distancia, quedan fuera de la superficie sólo por un lado de la pared y no por el otro;

VI. La pared fuere divisoria entre un edificio, del cual forma parte, y un jardín, campo, corral o sitio sin edificios;

VII. Un predio se halle cerrado o defendido por vallados, cercas o setos vivos y las contiguas no lo estén;

VIII. La cerca que encierra completamente un predio, es de distinta especie de la que tiene la vecina en sus lados contiguos a la primera; y

Article 978.- Indications contrary to co-ownership exist when:

I. There are windows or apertures opened in the dividing wall of the buildings;

II. All of the wall, barbed wire, fence, or shrubs are obviously constructed on a lot belonging to one of the properties, and not ***straddling*** the two adjoining ***lots***;

III. The wall supports the loads and runs, weights, and framing of one of the properties, and not of the adjoining ***property***;

IV. The dividing wall between patios, gardens, and other properties is constructed in such a way that the protective cap on top of the wall comes down in the direction of only one of the properties;

V. A dividing wall constructed of masonry featuring so-called stepping stones **[protruding bricks or stones that can act as crude steps]**, spanning a distance, which stand out from the surface on one side of the wall and not the other;

VI. The wall is a boundary between a building, of which it forms a part, and a garden, field, animal enclosure, or an area without buildings;

VII. A property is found to be blocked off or protected by barbed wire, fences, or hedges, and the adjoining ***properties*** are not;

VIII. The fence that completely surrounds a property is of a different type from the one that the neighbour owns on the sides adjoining ***this first property***; and

IX. Los materiales empleados en una estructura de edificación sean uniformes.

Artículo 979. En general, en los casos señalados en el artículo anterior, se presume que la propiedad de las paredes, cercas, vallados o setos, pertenece exclusivamente al dueño de la finca o predio que tiene a su favor estos signos exteriores.

Artículo 980. Las zanjas o acequias abiertas entre las heredades, se presumen también de copropiedad si no hay título o signo que demuestren lo contrario.

Artículo 981. Hay signo contrario a la copropiedad, cuando la tierra o broza sacada de la zanja o acequia para abrirla o limpiarla, se halla sólo de un lado; en este caso, se presume que la propiedad de la zanja o acequia es exclusivamente del dueño del predio sobre el cual se ha echado la tierra o broza.

Artículo 982. La presunción que establece el artículo anterior cesa, cuando la inclinación del terreno obliga a echar la tierra de un solo lado.

Artículo 983. Los dueños de los predios están obligados a cuidar de que no se deteriore la pared, zanja o seto de propiedad común; y si por el hecho de alguno de sus dependientes, animales, substancias almacenadas o producidas que sean corrosivas o inflamables, por maquinaria ahí emplazada, o por cualquiera otra causa que dependa de ellos, se deterioraren, deben reponerlos, pagando los daños y perjuicios que se hubieren causado.

IX. The materials used in a building structure are uniform.

Article 979.- In general, for the cases indicated in the previous article, it is presumed that the ownership of the walls, fences, barbed wire, or hedges belongs exclusively to the owner of the property or lot that has these outward indications in their favour.

Article 980.- Ditches or irrigation trenches opened between the **properties** are also presumed to be co-owned, if there is no title or indication that proves the opposite.

Article 981.- There is an indication contrary to co-ownership when the dirt or debris removed from a ditch or irrigation trench to open or clean it is found only on one **property**. In this case, it is presumed that the ownership of the ditch or irrigation trench is exclusive to the owner of the property on which the dirt or debris has been dumped.

Article 982.- The presumption that brings about the previous article ceases when the slope of the land has forced the dirt to be dumped on one **property**.

Article 983.- The owners of the properties are required to make sure that the common property wall, ditch, or hedge does not deteriorate; and if **the common property wall, ditch, or hedge** is damaged by an act of any of their dependants, animals, stored or produced substances which might be corrosive or inflammable, by machinery located **on their property**, or by any other cause relating to them, **the one causing the damage** must restore it, paying **for** the damages and losses they have caused.

Artículo 984. La reparación y reconstrucción de las paredes de propiedad común y el mantenimiento de los vallados, setos vivos, zanjas o acequias, también comunes, se costearán proporcionalmente por todos los dueños que tengan a su favor la copropiedad.

Artículo 985. El copropietario que quiera librarse de las obligaciones que impone el artículo anterior, puede hacerlo renunciando a la copropiedad, salvo el caso en que la pared común sostenga un edificio suyo.

Artículo 986. El propietario de un edificio que se apoye en una pared común, puede, al derribarlo, renunciar o no a la copropiedad. En el primer caso serán de su cuenta todos los gastos necesarios para evitar o reparar los daños que cause la demolición. En el segundo, además de ésta obligación, queda sujeto a las que le imponen los **artículos 983 y 984**.

Artículo 987. El propietario de una finca contigua a una pared divisoria que no sea común, sólo puede darle este carácter en todo o en parte, por contrato con el dueño de ella.

Artículo 988. Todo propietario puede alzar la pared de propiedad común, haciéndolo a sus expensas e indemnizando de los perjuicios que se ocasionen por la obra, aunque sean temporales.

Artículo 989. Serán igualmente de su cuenta todas las obras de conservación de la pared en la parte en donde esta haya aumentado su altura o espesor, así como las que en la parte común sean necesarias, siempre que el deterioro provenga de la mayor altura o espesor que se haya dado a la pared.

Article 984.- The repair and rebuilding of the common property walls, and the maintenance of the common fences, hedges, ditches, or irrigation trenches, must be paid proportionally by all the owners who **share in** the co-ownership.

Article 985.- A co-owner who wants to free himself from the obligations imposed by the previous article, can do so by renouncing co-ownership, except in the case where a common wall supports their own building.

Article 986.- The owner of a building that is supported by a common wall, when demolishing **the building**, can give up the co-ownership, or not. In the first case, all the necessary expenses to prevent or repair damages **to the common wall** caused by the demolition must be paid **by the owner who is demolishing the building**. In the second case, they remain liable for the **repair and maintenance** imposed by **Articles 983 and 984**.

Article 987.- The owner of a property adjoining a dividing wall that is not **a** common **wall,** can only be given this **right of co-ownership,** all or in part, by a contract with the owner **of the wall**.

Article 988.- Each owner can add onto a common property wall at their own expense, and compensating **the others** for any **losses or damages** caused by the work, even if the **losses or damages** are temporary.

Article 989.- Likewise, **an owner must** pay for all maintenance work for the part of the wall that they increased in height or thickness, as well as the necessary **expenses** for the common part, provided that the deterioration **requiring maintenance** results from the increased height or thickness given to the wall.

Artículo 990. Si la pared de propiedad común no puede resistir a la elevación, el propietario que quiera levantarla tendrá la obligación de reconstruirla a su costa, y si fuere necesario darle mayor espesor, deberá darlo de su suelo.

Article 990.- If the common property wall cannot be made higher **[because of its construction]**, the owner who wants to raise the height must re-build *the wall* at their expense, and, if it becomes necessary to increase the thickness, *the extra thickness* must come from their property.

Artículo 991. En los casos de aumento de la altura o del espesor de la barda, la pared continúa siendo de propiedad común hasta la altura que lo era antiguamente, aun cuando haya sido edificada de nuevo a expensas de uno solo; y desde el punto donde comenzó la mayor altura o mayor espesor, es propiedad de quien la edificó.

Article 991.- In the case of an increase in height or thickness, the wall continues to be co-owned up to the original height, even though it has been newly built at the expense of only one *owner*; and from the point where the greater height or thickness begins, it belongs to the owner who constructed *the changes*.

Artículo 992. Los demás propietarios que no hayan contribuido a dar más elevación o espesor a la pared, podrán, sin embargo, adquirir en la parte nuevamente elevada los derechos de copropiedad, pagando proporcionalmente el valor de la obra y la mitad del valor del terreno sobre que se hubiere dado mayor espesor.

Article 992.- The rest of the owners that have not contributed to the increased height or thickness can, at the same time, acquire a share of the newly constructed *section*, by paying proportionally the cost of the work, plus one-half of the value of the property on which an increased thickness *rests*.

Artículo 993. Cada copropietario de una pared común podrá usar de ella en proporción al derecho que tenga en la comunidad; podrá por tanto edificar, apoyando su obra en la pared común o introduciendo vigas hasta la mitad de su espesor, pero sin impedir el uso común y respectivo de los demás copropietarios. En caso de resistencia se arreglarán por medio de peritos las condiciones necesarias para que la nueva obra no perjudique los derechos de aquellos.

Article 993.- Each co-owner of a common wall can make use of it in proportion to the right that they have in the partnership **[of co-owners]**; they can, therefore, construct works attached to the common wall, or introduce beams *into the wall* up to one-half its thickness, but without interfering with the other owners' ordinary and proper use *of the wall*. In the case of opposition *to this construction*, an agreement must be reached by using experts *to determine* the necessary conditions so that the new work does not harm the rights of the others.

Artículo 994. Los árboles existentes en cerca de copropiedad o que señalen lindero, son también de copropiedad; estos no pueden ser cortados ni sustituidos con otros sin el consentimiento de ambos copropietarios o por decisión judicial pronunciada en juicio contradictorio, en caso de desacuerdo de los copropietarios.

Article 994.- Existing trees close to the joint property, or that mark a boundary, are also co-owned; these cannot be cut ***down*** or replaced without the consent of both co-owners, or, in the case of a disagreement of the co-owners, by a judicial decision handed down in a contested proceeding **[an adversarial hearing before a judge to determine the merit of a certain position]**.

Artículo 995. Los frutos del árbol o del arbusto común y los gastos de su cultivo, serán repartidos por partes iguales entre los copropietarios.

Article 995.- The fruit from the tree or common plant, and the expenses for its cultivation, must be shared equally between the co-owners.

Artículo 996. Ningún copropietario puede, sin consentimiento del otro, abrir ventanas ni hueco alguno en pared común.

Article 996.- No co-owner can, without the consent of the other, open any windows or apertures in a common wall.

Artículo 997. La copropiedad cesa: por la división del bien común; por la destrucción o pérdida de él; por su enajenación y por la consolidación o reunión de todas las partes alícuotas en un solo titular.

Article 997.- Co-ownership ends: by the division of the common property; by the destruction or loss of it; by transfer of ownership; and by the consolidation or re-uniting of all pro-rated parts ***of the co-owned asset*** into a single title.

Artículo 998. La división de una cosa común no perjudica a tercero.

Article 998.- The division of a ***common property*** cannot harm a third party.

Artículo 999. La división de bienes inmuebles es nula si no se hace con las mismas formalidades que la ley exige para su venta.

Article 999.- The division of real estate is nullified if it is not done with the same formalities that the law demands of a sale **[including a registered public document]**.

Artículo 1000. Son aplicables a la división entre copartícipes las reglas concernientes a la partición hereditaria.

Article 1000.- The rules concerning hereditary division **[inheritance laws]** are applicable to the division amongst ***co-owners***.

PART 5 – Obligations of Neighbours

Civil Code of the State of Jalisco
Book 3 – Title 13
Articles 1228 – 1251

Relevance to a Condominium

As well as the rights and obligations given to owners by the condo law in the Jalisco Civil Code (see "***Part 3 – The Jalisco Condo Law***"), your condo's by-laws, and the code section on co-ownership (see "***Part 4 – Co-Ownership***"), there's one more section of the Civil Code that applies to the rights and obligations of neighbours in general.

This includes rules about planting trees that interfere with a neighbour's property, owning bothersome animals, draining rainwater onto a neighbour's property, and more.

Every home owner or occupant of a property in Jalisco is bound by these rules, whether they live in a condo or not.

Versions of Laws Used

Codes and laws are living documents that are amended frequently by the level of government that issued them.

This section contains an excerpt from the *Código Civil del Estado de Jalisco* (Civil Code of the State of Jalisco), that took effect on **September 14, 1995**, and was last amended on ***December 20, 2014***.

Sections of the Laws Used

The excerpt from the **Jalisco Civil Code** translated in this section is from: *Libro Tercero – Título Decimotercero*:

Libro Tercero (Book Three) is titled "*De los bienes, su propiedad y sus diferentes manifestaciones*" (Property, Its Ownership, and Its Different Forms).

Título Decimotercero (Title Thirteen) is titled "*De los derechos y obligaciones de la vecindad*" (Rights and Obligations of Neighbours).

CÓDIGO CIVIL DEL ESTADO DE JALISCO	CIVIL CODE OF THE STATE OF JALISCO

CÓDIGO CIVIL DEL ESTADO DE JALISCO

LIBRO TERCERO

TÍTULO DECIMOTERCERO – DE LOS DERECHOS Y OBLIGACIONES DE LA VECINDAD

CAPÍTULO UNICO

Artículo 1228.- Todo propietario o poseedor, debe respetar el derecho que tienen los vecinos para usar y disfrutar de los predios y construcciones que ocupe.

Artículo 1229.- En zonas habitacionales y en edificios de vivienda múltiple deberá respetarse íntegramente el derecho de los vecinos a la paz y a la tranquilidad. Por ello no podrán tenerse en esas zonas animales que aun con el carácter de domésticos causen molestias y temor a los vecinos, ni tampoco operar aparatos de sonido o receptores de imágenes a volúmenes altos y que sean captados fuera del recinto en que se encuentren.

CIVIL CODE OF THE STATE OF JALISCO

BOOK THREE

TITLE THIRTEEN – RIGHTS AND OBLIGATIONS OF NEIGHBOURS

ONLY CHAPTER – Obligations of Neighbours

Article 1228.- Every owner or occupant must respect the right that their neighbours have to use and enjoy the land and buildings *these neighbours* occupy.

Article 1229.- In residential zones, and in multiple residence buildings **[such as apartments]**, the right of neighbours to peace and tranquillity must be thoroughly respected. Because of this, *neighbours* cannot have animals in these zones that, even when classified as domestic, cause bother and fear for their neighbours, nor to operate sound equipment or televisions at high volumes which can be heard outside of the enclosed area in which they are located. **[There are also maximum noise limits published by the *Secretaría de Medio Ambiente y Recursos Naturales* (Department of the Environment and Natural Resources) as *NORMA Oficial Mexicana NOM-081-ECOL-1994*]**

Artículo 1230.- El propietario, el usufructuario y el inquilino de un predio tienen derecho de ejercer las acciones que procedan para impedir que por el mal uso, o el abandono de la propiedad del vecino, se perjudiquen la seguridad, el sosiego o la salud de los que habiten el predio.

Article 1230.- The owner, the usufructuary **[a person who has the right to use and profit from a property owned by another – usually because of a contract]**, and the tenant of a property, have the right to take appropriate action to prevent misuse or abandonment of a neighbour's property when this would be detrimental to the safety, peace, or health of those who reside on the property **[on which the owner, usufructuary, or tenant reside]**.

Artículo 1231.- En un predio, no pueden hacerse excavaciones o construcciones que hagan perder el sostén necesario al suelo de la propiedad vecina; a menos que se hagan las obras de consolidación indispensables para evitar todo daño a éstas.

Article 1231.- Excavations or construction cannot be carried out on a property that will cause the loss of needed support for the soil of a neighbouring property; unless the necessary reinforcement work is done to prevent any damage to *this support*.

Artículo 1232.- Tampoco es permitido arrojar basura o depositarla en áreas comunes, banquetas o jardines ni aun en los propios.

Article 1232.- Discarding garbage, or depositing it onto common areas, sidewalks, or gardens, is forbidden; even on one's own *property*.

Artículo 1233.- Los recipientes donde se guarden las basuras y demás desechos deberán estar debidamente cerrados para evitar los efectos contaminantes del aire.

Article 1233.- Receptacles where garbage and other litter is stored, must be properly closed to prevent the effects of air contamination.

Artículo 1234.- A fin de conservar la armonía arquitectónica, queda prohibido en edificios de vivienda comunal o destinados a actividades comerciales o profesionales:

Article 1234.- To preserve architectural harmony, *the following* are prohibited in residential buildings, or in those intended for commercial or professional activities:

I. Cuando sean visibles, pintar el interior de los mismos e implementar cortinas que desentonen con el conjunto;

I. When visible, painting the inside and hanging curtains that clash with the rest of those in the building;

II. Tender ropa en los ventanales y terrazas o miradores;

II. Hanging up clothes in the windows and on terraces or balconies;

III. Obstruir los pasillos y áreas de circulación interior, aun con motivos estéticos;

III. Obstructing aisles and interior circulation areas, even for cosmetic reasons;

IV. Ocupar espacios comunes destinados al servicio de todos los vecinos como pueden ser patios, escaleras, estacionamientos, u otros similares; y

V. Agregar cualesquiera elementos que rompan la uniformidad arquitectónica.

Artículo 1235.- Todo propietario o poseedor deberá tener en perfecto funcionamiento sus ductos hidráulicos y de desalojo de aguas negras y pluviales.

Artículo 1236.- Todo propietario o poseedor deberá cuidar el perfecto y equilibrado funcionamiento de los sistemas de conducción de energía eléctrica; asimismo deberá contar con los sistemas de aislamiento y corte para evitar daños a las instalaciones de los vecinos.

Artículo 1237.- Es obligación de los propietarios y poseedores tener en buenas condiciones las instalaciones para el consumo de gas, debiendo estar los tanques en lugar fácilmente accesible y ventilado.

Artículo 1238.- No es lícito permitir la crianza ni la propagación de fauna cuando ésta represente un peligro para la salud humana o provoque molestias.

Artículo 1239.- Es obligación del propietario o poseedor de un predio, no permitir el paso hacia propiedades de vecinos a personas extrañas a ellas, y en su caso cuando adviertan su presencia en el vecindario reportarlas a las autoridades policíacas.

IV. Occupying common spaces intended to serve all residents such as patios, stairs, parking lots, or other similar items; and

V. Adding any elements that break the architectural uniformity.

Article 1235.- Every owner or occupant must keep their water, sewage, and rainwater pipes in perfect working order.

Article 1236.- Every owner or occupant must maintain perfect and balanced operation of *their* electrical systems; they must also have isolation and cut-off systems to prevent damage to a neighbour's facilities.

Article 1237.- It is the obligation of owners and occupants to keep gas facilities in good condition. Tanks must be in a place that is easily accessible and well-ventilated.

Article 1238.- It is not permissible to allow the breeding or propagation of animals when it poses a danger to human health, or causes annoyance *to neighbours*.

Article 1239.- It is the obligation of owners or occupants of a property to not allow passage into neighbouring properties to strangers, and, if they notice their presence in the neighbourhood, to report them to the police.

Artículo 1240.- Nadie puede plantar árboles cerca de un predio ajeno, sino a la distancia de dos metros de la línea divisoria, si la plantación se hace de árboles grandes; y de un metro, si la plantación se hace de arbustos o árboles pequeños.

Artículo 1241.- El propietario o poseedor puede pedir que se arranquen los árboles plantados a menor distancia de su predio de la señalada en el Artículo que precede; y aun cuando sea mayor, si es evidente el daño que los árboles causen.

Artículo 1242.- Si las ramas de los árboles se extienden sobre predios, jardines o patios vecinos, el dueño de éstos tendrá derecho de que se corten en cuanto se extiendan sobre su propiedad, y si fueren las raíces de los árboles las que se extendieren en el suelo del otro, éste podrá hacerlas cortar por sí mismo dentro de su heredad, pero con previo aviso al vecino.

Artículo 1243.- El dueño de una pared que no sea de copropiedad, contigua a finca ajena, puede abrir en ella ventanas o huecos para recibir luces, cumpliendo las disposiciones que sobre urbanización se dieren.

Artículo 1244.- Sin embargo, de lo dispuesto en el artículo anterior, el dueño de la finca o propiedad contigua a la pared en que estuvieren abiertas las ventanas o huecos, podrá construir pared contigua a ella, o si adquiere la copropiedad, apoyarse en la misma pared, aunque de uno u otro modo cubra los huecos o ventanas.

Article 1240.- No one can plant trees close to another's property. ***They must be*** at a distance of two meters from the property line, if the planting consists of large trees, and one meter, if the planting consists of shrubs and small trees.

Article 1241.- An owner or occupant can demand that trees planted within a lesser distance from their property line, as indicated in the previous article, be removed; even older ***trees***, if the damage that these trees cause is evident.

Article 1242.- If tree branches extend over adjoining properties, gardens, or patios, the owner of these ***affected properties*** has a right to cut them as soon as they extend over their property, and if the roots of the trees extend into the other's ground, they can cut them inside of their property, but ***must provide*** prior notice to the neighbour.

Article 1243.- The owner of a wall that is not co-owned, and adjoins someone else's property, can open windows or holes in ***this wall*** to let in light, in compliance with existing statutes covering urban development.

Article 1244.- Notwithstanding the previous article, the owner of the estate or property adjoining the wall in which the windows or holes have been opened, can construct a wall adjacent to ***this wall***, or, if they acquire co-ownership, abutting up against this same wall, despite the fact that, one way or another, ***this new wall*** will cover these holes or windows.

Artículo 1245.- No se pueden tener ventanas para asomarse ni balcones u otros voladizos semejantes, sobre la propiedad del vecino, prolongándose más allá del límite que separa las heredades. Tampoco pueden tenerse vistas de costado u oblicuas sobre la misma propiedad, si no hay un metro de distancia.

Article 1245.- It is forbidden to have protruding windows, balconies, or other similar overhanging construction, hanging over the property of a neighbour, extending beyond the boundary that separates the properties. It is also forbidden to have side or oblique views over the same property **[from windows or balconies]**, *unless* these are *at least* one meter distance *from the neighbouring property*.

Artículo 1246.- La distancia de que habla el artículo anterior se mide desde la línea de separación de las dos propiedades.

Article 1246.- The distance mentioned in the previous article is measured from the boundary between the two properties.

Artículo 1247.- No se podrán construir edificios que por su altura considerable traigan como consecuencia privar a los predios colindantes ya edificados, del aprovechamiento de los rayos solares.

Article 1247.- Buildings cannot be constructed which, because of their significant height, block the enjoyment of sunshine by neighbouring properties that are already built.

Artículo 1248.- El propietario de un edificio está obligado a construir sus tejados y azoteas de tal manera que las aguas pluviales no caigan sobre el suelo o edificio vecino.

Article 1248.- The owner of a building is obligated to construct their roofs and roof terraces in such a way that rainwater does not fall on the neighbouring ground or buildings.

Artículo 1249.- Nadie puede construir cerca de una pared ajena o de copropiedad, fosos, cloacas, acueductos, hornos, fraguas, chimeneas, establos; ni instalar depósitos de materias corrosivas, máquinas de vapor o fábricas destinadas a usos que puedan ser peligrosos o nocivos, sin guardar las distancias prescritas por los reglamentos o sin construir las obras de resguardo necesarias con sujeción a lo que prevengan los mismos reglamentos, o a falta de ellos, a lo que se determine por peritos.

Article 1249.- No one can construct close to someone else's *wall*, or to a co-owned wall, ditches, sewers, aqueducts, ovens, forges, chimneys, stables; nor set up dumps for corrosive materials, steam engines, or factories destined for uses that can be dangerous or harmful, without maintaining the distances prescribed by regulations, or without constructing the necessary protective works in accordance with that which is prescribed by the same regulations, or with a lack of *regulations*, that which is determined by authorities.

Artículo 1250.- Es obligación de los propietarios de predios sin construir dentro de las áreas urbanas, mantener aseados y bardar los mismos, para evitar se conviertan en depósitos de desechos y que se propicie la crianza de fauna nociva a la salud humana.

Artículo 1251.- Es obligación de los propietarios u ocupantes de fincas en áreas urbanas, asearlas y darles el mantenimiento adecuado, aun en el caso en que estén desocupadas.

Article 1250.- It is the obligation of owners of vacant land within urban areas, to keep them clean and not overgrown, to avoid them becoming waste dumps, and breeding wildlife harmful to human health **[such as rats or squirrels]**.

Article 1251.- It is the obligation of the owners or occupants of properties in urban areas to clean them, and give them proper maintenance, even if they are unoccupied **[cannot become dilapidated or run-down]**.

PART 6 – Legal Entities

Civil Code of the State of Jalisco Book 2 – Title 3 Articles 161 – 171

Relevance to Condominiums

Civil Code Article 161 lists 14 specific "legal persons." These aren't individuals, but legal entities specifically defined in the law, and governed by separate and specific sections of the Civil Code.

Of most interest to condo administrators and owners are **#12 – Condominiums** and **#9 – Associations**.

It's important to understand that these are two distinct and separate legal entities, and that they fall under separate sections of the Code. They aren't treated the same under the law.

> **Condominiums** are dealt with under *Libro Tercero – Titulo Sexto: Articles 1001-1038* (see **Part 3 – The Jalisco Condo Law** for a translation of this section).

> **Associations** are dealt with under *Libro Segundo – Titulo Tercero – Capitulo II: Articles 172-189* (see **Part 10 – Civil Associations (A.C.s)** for a translation of this section).

Articles 162 through 171 of the Civil Code go on to describe some general rules that apply to all non-individuals that are expressly named as legal entities (such as a condominium or an association).

Versions of Laws Used

Codes and laws are living documents that are amended frequently by the level of government that issued them.

This section contains an excerpt from the *Código Civil del Estado de Jalisco* (Civil Code of the State of Jalisco), that took effect on **September 14, 1995**, and was last amended on **December 20, 2014**.

Sections of the Laws Used

The excerpt from the **Jalisco Civil Code** translated in this section is from *Libro Segundo – Título Tercero*:

> *Libro Segundo* (Book Two) is titled *"De las personas y de las instituciones de familia"* (Persons and Family Entities).

> *Título Tercero* (Title Three) is titled *"De las personas jurídicas"* (Legal Entities).

CÓDIGO CIVIL DEL ESTADO DE JALISCO	CIVIL CODE OF THE STATE OF JALISCO

CÓDIGO CIVIL DEL ESTADO DE JALISCO

LIBRO SEGUNDO

TÍTULO TERCERO – DE LAS PERSONAS JURÍDICAS

CAPÍTULO I – DISPOSICIONES GENERALES

Artículo 161: Son personas jurídicas:

I. El Gobierno Federal, las partes integrantes de la Federación y los municipios;

II. Las corporaciones de carácter público reconocidas por la ley;

III. Los organismos descentralizados;

IV. Los partidos políticos reconocidos conforme a la legislación electoral;

V. Los sindicatos laborales y patronales;

VI. Las sociedades cooperativas y mutualistas;

VII. Los ejidos, las comunidades indígenas, las uniones de ejidos y demás entidades reguladas por las leyes agrarias;

CIVIL CODE OF THE STATE OF JALISCO

BOOK TWO

TITLE THREE – LEGAL ENTITIES

CHAPTER I – General Provisions [Legal Entities]

Article 161: These are legal persons **[legal entities]**:

I. The Federal Government, the constituent parts of the Federation, and the municipalities;

II. Public corporations recognised by law;

III. Decentralised organisations **[administrative units created by decree of Congress or the President, that produce goods and services to satisfy social needs and demands.]**;

IV. Recognised political parties, in accordance with electoral legislation;

V. Labour unions and employers;

VI. Cooperatives and mutual benefit societies **[a society designed specifically to help those in need in a community]**;

VII. The *ejidos* **[cooperative farming communities]**, indigenous communities, unions of *ejidos*, and other entities regulated by Agrarian Law;

VIII. Las sociedades civiles o mercantiles;

IX. Las asociaciones civiles;

X. Las fundaciones;

XI. Las asociaciones y órdenes religiosas;

XII. Los condominios;

XIII. Las personas jurídicas extranjeras, con autorización expresa para operar dentro del territorio del Estado; y

XIV. Las demás instituciones u organismos constituidos y reconocidos como personas jurídicas conforme a las leyes.

Artículo 162: Las personas jurídicas pueden ejercitar todos los derechos que no sean incompatibles con el objeto de su institución y en general todos aquellos que no les estén prohibidos por la ley.

Artículo 163: Las personas jurídicas se regirán por las leyes correspondientes, por su escritura constitutiva, por sus estatutos y se obligan por medio de los órganos que las representen legítimamente.

Artículo 164.- La denominación de las personas jurídicas se determina:

I. Por la ley que las haya creado o reconocido o que las rija directamente;

VIII. Nonprofit or business corporations [*sociedades anónimas* **such as an *S.A. de C.V.***];

IX. Civil associations **[A.C.s]**;

X. Foundations;

XI. Religious orders and religious associations;

XII. **Condominiums**;

XIII. Foreign legal entities **[such as a company]**, with the express authorisation to operate within the territory of the state; and

XIV. Other institutions or bodies formed and recognized as legal entities in accordance with the laws.

Article 162: Legal persons **[legal entities]** can exercise all rights that are consistent with the purpose of their establishment, and, in general, all those *rights* that are not prohibited by law **[such as a criminal act]**.

Article 163: Legal entities must abide by the corresponding laws **[there are laws specific to each type of legal entity]**, by their establishing document **[such as articles of incorporation, or a condo's *escritura constitutiva*]**, by their statutes, and obligate themselves by means of the bodies that legitimately represent them **[such as a Board]**.

Article 164.- The legal name of a legal entity is determined:

I. By the law that created or recognised it, or that governs it directly;

II. Por acuerdo de quienes expresamente las constituyan; y

III. Por los usos y tradiciones que les resulten.

Artículo 165.- La protección que la ley da al nombre de las personas físicas, se extiende a la denominación que corresponda a las personas jurídicas.

Artículo 166.- El domicilio de las personas jurídicas se determina:

I. Por la ley que las haya creado o reconocido, o las rija directamente;

II. Por su escritura constitutiva o sus estatutos sociales; y

III. Cuando no haya señalamiento expreso del domicilio, se tendrá por tal, el lugar en que ejerzan sus funciones principales o en el que se haya establecido su representación legal.

Artículo 167.- Las personas jurídicas por su origen y formación, se clasifican en públicas y privadas.

Artículo 168.- Son personas jurídicas públicas, aquéllas que son creadas por una disposición legislativa o por un acto administrativo de gobierno.

Artículo 169.- Son personas jurídicas privadas, aquéllas que tienen como origen un acto de carácter particular.

II. By specific agreement by those who make it up; and

III. By the uses and customary practices that result from it.

Article 165.- The protection that the law gives to the name of *individuals* extends to the legal name belonging to the legal entity.

Article 166.- The *location for legal purposes* of a legal entity is determined:

I. By the law that created or recognised it, or that governs it directly;

II. By its establishing document **[such as articles of incorporation]** or its statutes **[by-laws]**.

III. When there is no express indication of the *legal location*, it is considered to be the place where it carries out its main functions, or in which its legal representation is established.

Article 167.- Legal entities are classified as *either* public or private, based on their origin and function.

Article 168.- Public legal entities are those that are created by a legislative instrument, or by an administrative act of government.

Article 169.- Private legal entities are those that originate from a private action **[such as registering a company, forming an association, or creating a condo regime]**.

Artículo 170.- Las personas jurídicas privadas que tengan su domicilio fuera del Estado, que realizan regularmente actos o hechos jurídicos dentro del territorio de Jalisco, se tendrán como domiciliadas en el lugar donde éstos hubieren sido ejecutados, para todo lo relativo a los derechos y obligaciones que les competan.

Artículo 171.- Las personas jurídicas pueden pactar el establecimiento de domicilios convencionales, dentro y fuera del Estado, para el ejercicio de sus derechos y cumplimiento de obligaciones, así como la renuncia en el aspecto judicial a la jurisdicción de su domicilio.

Article 170.- For everything relating to the rights and obligations that pertain to them, private legal entities that have their *legal location* out of the state, *but* that regularly carry out actions or legal activities inside the territory of Jalisco, must have as their *legal location* the place where these *activities* are being carried out.

Article 171.- Legal entities can agree to set up an elected domicile **[an agreed address for legal purposes]**, inside and outside of the state, to exercise their rights and fulfil *their* obligations, as well as to renounce, in the legal sense, the jurisdiction of their *legal location*.

PART 7 – The Public Registry of Property

Civil Code of the State of Jalisco
Book 3 – Title 14
Articles 1252 – 1258,

Jalisco Code of Civil Procedures
Title Six
Articles 399 & 400
&
Public Registry of Property Law
Title Three
Articles 99 – 104

Relevance to Condominiums

For a condominium regime to be legally set up, or for a deed of sale for a house or apartment in a condominium to be legal, there must be an *escritura pública* (public document) registered in the local *Registro Público de la Propiedad* (Public Registry of Property). For the condo itself, this will be the *escritura constitutiva* that sets up the condo property as a condo regime.

The same applies to the minutes of all ordinary assemblies, and any extraordinary assemblies where resolutions are passed that have significant legal effects (such as a change to the condo's by-laws, or the decision to force the sale of a property belonging to a delinquent owner):

Ordinary assembly minutes must be registered so that the Council and Administrator have the legal right to act for the condo, and so that the budget and fees are binding on the owners.

To prove the legal authority of the Administrator to act on behalf of the condo, the registered document is needed for any lawsuit or administrative act (such as opening or changing a bank account).

To prove the legal basis for the condo fees, the registered document is needed to sue a delinquent owner.

Extraordinary assembly minutes must be registered so that the resolutions passed by the assembly are binding. The registered document is needed to support any legal action arising from these decisions.

Most lawsuits will require copies of all changes to the by-laws.

A lawsuit to force the sale of a condo unit will require a copy of the registered minutes of the extraordinary assembly where this action was decided.

This section contains portions of the law that makes all such registered public documents binding on third parties, their ability to be used as evidence in a lawsuit, and how the registry can freeze the property record as a precautionary measure when the condo has forced a property to be sold because of delinquencies.

Versions of Laws Used

Codes and laws are living documents that are amended frequently by the level of government that issued them.

This section contains excerpts from:

the *Código Civil del Estado de Jalisco* (Civil Code of the State of Jalisco), that took effect on **September 14, 1995**, and was last amended on *December 20, 2014*;

the *Código de Procedimientos Civiles del Estado de Jalisco* (Code of Civil Procedures of the State of Jalisco), that took effect on **January 1, 1939**, and was last amended on *November 29, 2014*; and

the *Ley del Registro Público de la Propiedad del Estado del Jalisco* (Public Registry of Property Law), that took effect on **May 4, 2001**, and was last amended on *January 23, 2007*.

Sections of the Laws Used

The excerpt from the **Jalisco Civil Code** translated in this section is *Libro Tercero – Título Decimocuarto*:

Libro Tercero (Book Three) is titled *"De los bienes, su propiedad y sus diferentes manifestaciones"* (Property, Its Ownership, and Its Different Forms).

Título Decimocuarto (Title Fourteen) is titled *"Del Registro Público de la Propiedad"* (The Public Registry of Property).

The excerpt from the **Jalisco Code of Civil Procedures** translated in this section is from *Título Sexto*:

Título Sexto (Title Six) is titled *"Del Juicio Ordinario"* (The Ordinary Lawsuit).

The excerpt from the **Public Registry of Property Law** translated in this section is from *Título Tercero*:

Título Tercero (Title Three) is untitled.

CÓDIGO CIVIL DEL ESTADO DE JALISCO	CIVIL CODE OF THE STATE OF JALISCO

LIBRO TERCERO

BOOK THREE

TÍTULO DECIMOCUARTO – DEL REGISTRO PÚBLICO DE LA PROPIEDAD

TITLE FOURTEEN – THE PUBLIC REGISTRY OF PROPERTY

CAPÍTULO ÚNICO

ONLY CHAPTER – Public Registry of Property

Artículo 1252.- Mediante el Registro Público de la Propiedad se da publicidad a los actos jurídicos que conforme a la ley precisan de ese requisito para surtir efectos contra terceros.

Article 1252.- By law, legal acts must be published **[registered]** in the *Registro Público de la Propiedad* (Public Registry Of Property) to become effective against third parties.

Artículo 1253.- Los actos que siendo registrables no se registren, sólo producirán efectos entre quienes lo celebren, pero no podrán producir perjuicios a terceros, quienes los podrán aprovechar en todo tiempo.

Article 1253.- Acts that are recordable, but are not registered, can only ***have legal effect*** between those who ***carry them out***, who can benefit from them at all times, but ***these acts*** cannot bring about damages **[legal effects]** to third parties.

Artículo 1254.- Las inscripciones hechas en el Registro Público de la Propiedad tienen efectos declarativos y no constitutivos, de tal manera que los derechos provienen del acto jurídico declarado, pero no de su inscripción, cuya finalidad es dar publicidad y no constituir el derecho.

Article 1254.- Registrations made in the Public Registry Of Property have declaratory effects, and not establishing ***ones***, therefore the rights come from the declared legal act ***itself***, and not from its registration. The purpose of ***registration*** is ***publishing*** the act, and not creating the right.

Artículo 1255.- No obstante lo dispuesto en el artículo anterior, los actos o contratos que se otorguen o celebren por personas que en el Registro Público de la Propiedad aparezcan con derechos para ello, no se invalidarán en cuanto a tercero de buena fe, una vez registrados, aunque después se anulen o se resuelva el derecho del otorgante en virtud del título anterior no inscrito o de causas que no resulten claramente del mismo registro.

Article 1255.- Notwithstanding the previous article, acts or contracts that are granted or executed by persons that appear in the Public Registry of Property with the rights to ***these acts or contracts***, cannot be invalidated in the case of a good faith third party, once registered, even after the grantor ***of the act or contract's*** right is cancelled or annulled by virtue of the previous nonregistered title, or by causes that do not clearly result from the same record.

Lo dispuesto en este artículo no se aplicará a los contratos gratuitos, ni a actos o contratos que se ejecuten u otorguen violando una ley prohibitiva o de interés público.

Artículo 1256.- No podrá ejercitarse acción alguna contradictoria del dominio de inmuebles o de derechos reales registrados a nombre de persona o entidad determinada, sin que previamente, o a la vez, se entable demanda de nulidad o cancelación del registro en que conste dicho dominio o derecho.

Artículo 1257.- No pueden aparecer los bienes raíces o derechos reales impuestos sobre los mismos, inscritos a la vez en favor de dos o más personas distintas, a menos que éstas sean copartícipes.

Artículo 1258.- La preferencia entre derechos que sean registrables sobre un mismo bien, se determina en la siguiente forma:

I. Tratándose de derechos reales, por la prioridad en su registro independientemente de cuándo se hubieren adquirido siempre que la controversia se de entre adquirentes de la misma calidad.

La afectación de bienes en fideicomiso se equipara a una trasmisión de derechos reales;

The provisions of this article do not apply to gratuitous contracts **[contracts with no obvious goal or result]**, or to acts or contracts that have been fulfilled **[completed]**, or that violate a prohibitive law **[a law which explicitly prohibits some act]** or the public interest.

Article 1256.- No one can take any action contradictory to the **control and use** of real estate or real rights that have been registered on behalf of a person or a defined **legal** entity, without previously, or at the same time, establishing a claim of invalidity or cancellation of the record of the aforementioned control or **real** right.

Article 1257.- It is not possible for real estate, or real rights pertaining to them, to be registered in favour of two or more different people at the same time, unless they are joint partners **[co-owners]**.

Article 1258.- Preference between rights that can be registered on the same asset is decided in the following manner:

I. In the matter of real rights **[legal relationship between a person and one or more physical objects]**, by the precedence in the registration record, regardless of when they were acquired, provided that the dispute is between buyers of the same type.

The allocation of assets in a trust is considered equal to a transfer of real rights;

II. Tratándose de controversias sobre derechos reales, entre un adquirente a título oneroso y un adquirente a título gratuito, prevalecerá el derecho de quien lo hizo a título oneroso, independientemente de la fecha de su registro siempre que su adquisición se hiciere con anterioridad;

III. Tratándose de controversias entre adquirentes de derechos reales a título oneroso y el adquirente de derechos personales, prevalecerá el del titular del derecho real, independientemente de la época de su inscripción en el Registro, con la condición de que su adquisición sea anterior a la inscripción del derecho personal;

IV. Si la controversia fuere entre el adquirente del derecho real a título gratuito frente a un adquirente de derecho personal, prevalecerá la de éste último siempre que fuere inscrito con anterioridad a la que motiva el derecho real; y

V. Cuando la controversia sea entre adquirentes de derechos personales, la preferencia se determinará por la prioridad en su registro, independientemente de la época de su adquisición.

II. In the matter of disputes over real rights that were acquired by one party as a gift, and by another as a purchase, the right of the purchased title must prevail, regardless of the date of its registration, provided that it was acquired first;

III. In the matter of disputes between parties that acquire real rights by purchase, and an acquirer of personal rights **[legal relationship between a person and an abstract thing or a human act]**, the real right must prevail, regardless of the age of its registration in the registration record, provided that it was purchased before the registration of the personal right;

IV. If the dispute was between a party that was gifted a real right and an acquirer of a personal right, this last **[acquirer of a personal right]** must prevail provided that it was registered before the *act* that gave rise to the real right; and

V. When the dispute is between acquirers of personal rights, preference is determined by the precedence of registration *of the right*, regardless of the age of its acquisition.

CÓDIGO DE PROCEDIMIENTOS CIVILES DEL ESTADO DE JALISCO

TÍTULO SEXTO – DEL JUICIO ORDINARIO

CAPÍTULO V – Del Valor de las Pruebas

Artículo 399.- Los instrumentos públicos hacen prueba plena, aunque se presenten sin citación del colitigante, salvo siempre el derecho de éste para redargüirlos de falsedad y para pedir su cotejo con los protocolos y archivos. En caso de inconformidad con el protocolo o archivo, los instrumentos no tendrán valor probatorio en el punto en que existiere la inconformidad.

Artículo 400.- Los instrumentos públicos no se perjudicarán en cuanto a su validez por las excepciones que se aleguen para destruir la acción que en ellos se funde; y no podrán objetarse sino con otros posteriores de la misma especie, salvo el caso de simulación en el que se podrá hacer uso de cualquier otro medio de prueba

CODE OF CIVIL PROCEDURES OF THE STATE OF JALISCO

TITLE SIX – THE ORDINARY LAWSUIT

CHAPTER V – The Value of Evidence

Article 399.- Public documents are conclusive evidence, even if they are presented without citing the co-litigant, always maintaining the **co-litigant's** right to contest their validity, and to request a comparison with protocols and records. In the case of a disagreement with the protocol or the record, the document cannot have value as evidence at the point *in the document* where the nonconformity occurs.

Article 400.- The validity of public documents cannot be damaged by exceptions that are alleged to defeat the action that is established in *these documents*; and *those contesting the documents* cannot simply raise objections with other subsequent *documents* of the same type, except in the case of simulation **[agreement by two or more persons to give one thing the appearance of another for the purpose of fraud]**, in which case, *those contesting the documents* can make use of any other evidence.

<u>**LEY DEL REGISTRO PÚBLICO DE LA PROPIEDAD DEL ESTADO DEL JALISCO**</u>	<u>**LAW OF THE PUBLIC REGISTRY OF PROPERTY OF THE STATE OF JALISCO**</u>

<u>**TÍTULO TERCERO (SIN TÍTULO)**</u>

<u>**TITLE THREE (UNTITLED)**</u>

CAPÍTULO VIII – De los Avisos Cautelar y Preventivo

CHAPTER VIII – Preventative and Precautionary Notices

Artículo 99. El notario, autoridad o titular registral podrá solicitar la inmovilidad registral, cuando vaya a celebrar un acto jurídico por el cual se declare, reconozca, adquiera, transmita, modifique, limite, grave o extinga la propiedad o posesión de bienes raíces o cualquier derecho real sobre los mismos o que sin serlo sea objeto de registro, cumpliendo las siguientes condiciones:

Article 99. The *notario* (civil law notary), authority, or registered titleholder can request the ***freezing of the public record***, when ***this request*** is made to carry out a judicial act in which was declared, acknowledged, acquired, transmitted, modified, limited, taxed, or extinguished the ownership or possession of real estate, or any real right over the same, or that without being recorded, is the subject of registration, must comply with the following conditions:

I. El notario, autoridad o titular registral, podrán solicitar a la institución, la inmovilidad por un término máximo de cuarenta y cinco días hábiles a partir de su expedición, lo que podrá realizarse a través del sistema informático. En caso de que la solicitud sea presentada por el titular registral, ésta deberá de realizarse por escrito ratificado ante notario; y

I. The *notario*, authority, or registered titleholder can request from the ***registry***, the ***freezing of the public record*** for a maximum period of forty-five **[45]** working days from the issuance ***of the judicial act***, which can be carried out by means of an information-technology system. If the application is presented by the registered titleholder, ***the request*** must be made by ***means of*** a written document ratified by a *notario*; and

II. Deberá señalar respecto de la operación que pretende llevar a cabo:

II. ***The following*** must be indicated regarding the proceeding that is intended to come about **[in the legal document]**:

a) Naturaleza del acto jurídico;

a) the nature of the judicial act;

b) Nombre de los contratantes; e

b) the names of the parties involved; and

c) Inmueble materia de la operación, señalando sus antecedentes registrales.

c) the real estate property that is the subject of the proceeding, indicating its archival antecedents **[history of property ownership]**.

Artículo 100.- El Registrador anotará de inmediato la solicitud a que se refiere el artículo anterior, señalando día y hora de la presentación y expedirá al interesado un certificado que incluya el aviso cautelar, con sus limitaciones y gravámenes si los hubiere.

Article 100. The Registrar **[official at the Public Registry]** must immediately record the application referred to in the previous article, indicating the day and time of the presentation, and will issue to the applicant a certificate that includes the preventative notice, along with its limitations and any liens that might exist.

Artículo 101.- Los efectos de la inmovilidad registral, no producen ningún derecho contractual y durarán cuarenta y cinco días hábiles, contados a partir del día y hora de la expedición del aviso ante el registrador, término que se debe considerar adicionalmente al que concede el aviso preventivo regulado en la Ley del Notariado.

Article 101. The effects of the ***freezing of the public record*** do not produce any contractual rights, and they can last for forty-five **[45]** working days from the day and hour of the issuance of the notice before the Registrar, a period that should be considered as additional to that which is granted to the preventative notice regulated by the Notarial Law.

Artículo 102.- Si durante la vigencia del aviso cautelar, y en relación con la misma finca o derechos, se presenta otro documento contradictorio para su registro, éste último será objeto de una anotación preventiva, a fin de que adquiera la prelación que le corresponda, en caso de que se opere la cancelación o caducidad de alguna anotación anterior en caso contrario las anotaciones preventivas de dichos documentos quedarán sin efecto.

Article 102. If, during the term of the preventative notice, and relating to the same property or rights, another contradictory document is presented for this record, this ***new document*** must be the subject of a cautionary annotation, on which basis it will acquire the priority that corresponds to it, in the event that it is removed by the cancellation or expiry of any previous annotation, otherwise the cautionary annotations of said documents will remain null and void.

Artículo 103.- Si se presenta el testimonio respectivo para su registro dentro de los términos que señalan los artículos anteriores, surtirá efecto contra terceros desde el día y hora de la presentación del aviso cautelar siempre y cuando exista identidad entre el aviso y la operación celebrada.

Article 103. If a testimony **[official notarial document]** is presented regarding this record within the time period indicated in the previous articles, it will come into effect against third parties, starting from the day and time of the presentation of the preventative notice, if and when the proceeding to be carried out and the notice are the same.

Si el documento se presenta para su registro con posterioridad al término establecido en el presente artículo, su registro sólo surtirá efectos desde la fecha de la presentación.

If the document is presented for registration after the time established in this article, its registration will only yield legal effects starting from the date of its presentation.

Artículo 104.- Cuando se firme una escritura en la que se declare, reconozca, adquiera, transmita, modifique, limite, grave o extinga la propiedad o posesión de bienes raíces o cualquier derecho real sobre los mismos o que sin serlo sea registrable el notario que la autorice dará a la Institución, a mas tardar dentro de los dos días hábiles siguientes a aquel en que se haya firmado la escritura, por escrito o cualquier otro medio indubitable, un aviso preventivo en el que conste la indicación del acto jurídico celebrado respecto al inmueble de que se trata, describiéndolo con su superficie, medidas lineales, colindancias, clave y cuenta catastral municipal y demás datos de identificación, así como los nombres de los interesados en la operación, señalando sus generales; en el caso de existir sociedad legal o conyugal, el nombre del cónyuge y el régimen legal; la fecha de la escritura, y la fecha de su firma con la indicación del número y sección en que estuviere inscrita la propiedad en la Institución.

Article 104. When a public document is signed in which was declared, acknowledged, acquired, transmitted, modified, limited, taxed, or extinguished the ownership or possession of real estate, or any real right over the same, or, without being recordable, the *notario* that authorised it must give to the Registry, at the latest within two **[2]** working days following the date on which the public document was signed, in writing, or by any other indisputable means, a preventative notice in which is recorded the instructions from the judicial act in relation to the real estate property in question, describing it, including its area, linear measurements, boundaries, key elements, and municipal tax account **number**, and all other identification data, as well as the names of the interested parties in the proceeding, showing their personal data; in the case of there being a legal partnership **[marriage]** or a conjugal partnership **[unmarried couple]**, the spouse's name, and the legal status *of the partnership*; the date of the public document, and the date it was signed, with an indication of the number and section in which the property is recorded in the Registry.

PART 8 – Powers of Attorney & Proxies

Federal Civil Code
Book Four Part 2 – Title Nine
Article 2554
&
Civil Code of the
State of Jalisco
Book Five – Title Nine
Articles 2197 to 2216

Relevance to a Condominium

There are many situations where the power to act on behalf of the condo must be given to someone, or when someone has been given the power to act on behalf of an owner to carry out condo business involving that owner's condo rights (percentage share in the common property).

The Administrator is given the power by the Civil Code to act for the condo by **Article 1012**, and the Council (Board) by **Article 1017**. For legal purposes, however, these powers must also be formalised in the registered minutes of the ordinary assembly in which the Administrator is appointed and the Council elected. A copy of these registered minutes will be needed for most lawsuits and administrative actions. These minutes are treated by the court as if they were a power of attorney.

Article 1017 of the Civil Code also gives the Council the power to authorise the Administrator to give powers to act for the condo to anyone needed to defend and carry out the interests of the Condo. These might be needed for any number of reasons (for example, this person could be a lawyer).

Proxies for assembly voting are also a type of power of attorney.

In the case of a foreign owner who bought their property through a bank trust, a powers of attorney is often given by the trust bank to let the owner, or a third party of the owner's choice, vote at a condo assembly. In this case, a proxy is not sufficient.

Powers of attorney are usually called *poders* or *mandatos*. The types of powers of attorney are described in **Article 2204**. Proxies normally fall under section III of this article.

Article 2554 of the Federal Civil Code is included because it must be quoted in any power of attorney prepared by a *notario* (civil law notary).

For more information on what constitutes a legal signature, and the validity of signed documents transmitted by fax or email, see "***Part 9 – Legal Signatures & Electronic Transmissions***."

For more information on how to use proxies at condo assemblies, and the form these must take, see our companion book, the "***Jalisco Condo Manual – Second Edition***."

Versions of Laws Used

Codes and laws are living documents that are amended frequently by the level of government that issued them.

This section contains excerpts from:

the *Código Civil Federal* (Federal Civil Code), that took effect on **August 31, 1928**, and was last amended on ***December 24, 2013***; and

the *Código Civil del Estado de Jalisco* (Civil Code of the State of Jalisco), that took effect on **September 14, 1995**, and was last amended on ***December 20, 2014.***

Sections of the Laws Used

The excerpt from the **Federal Civil Code** translated in this section is *Libro Cuarto – Parte Segundo – Título Noveno*:

Libro Cuarto – Parte Segundo (Book Four – Part 2) is titled *"De las diversas especies de contratos"* (The Various Types of Contracts).

Título Noveno (Title Nine) is titled *"Del Mandato"* (Directives).

The excerpt from the **Jalisco Civil Code** translated in this section is *Libro Quinto – Título Noveno*:

Libro Quinto (Book Five) is untitled *"De las diversas especies de contratos"* (The Various Types of Contracts).

Título Noveno (Title Nine) is titled *"Del Mandato"* (Directives).

Translation Note

These code sections both deal with *El Mandato*. In a legal sense, this translates literally as a **"directive"**, **"order"**, **"warrant"**, **"writ"**, or **"summons"**.

In the context of these sections, the **intent** is a **"directive for representation,"** and is better translated into English as a **"power of attorney."** So, that's what is used throughout this translation.

<u>**CÓDIGO CIVIL FEDERAL**</u>	<u>**FEDERAL CIVIL CODE**</u>

<u>**LIBRO CUATRO**</u>

<u>**PARTE SEGUNDO – DE LAS DIVERSAS ESPECIES DE CONTRATOS**</u>

<u>**TÍTULO NOVENO – DEL MANDATO**</u>

CAPÍTULO I – Dispsiciones Generales

Artículo 2554.- En todos los poderes generales para pleitos y cobranzas, bastará que se diga que se otorga con todas las facultades generales y las especiales que requieran cláusula especial conforme a la ley, para que se entiendan conferidos sin limitación alguna.

En los poderes generales para administrar bienes, bastará expresar que se dan con ese carácter, para que el apoderado tenga toda clase de facultades administrativas.

En los poderes generales, para ejercer actos de dominio, bastará que se den con ese carácter para que el apoderado tenga todas las facultades de dueño, tanto en lo relativo a los bienes, como para hacer toda clase de gestiones a fin de defenderlos.

Cuando se quisieren limitar, en los tres casos antes mencionados, las facultades de los apoderados, se consignarán las limitaciones, o los poderes serán especiales.

Los notarios insertarán este artículo en los testimonios de los poderes que otorguen.

<u>**BOOK FOUR**</u>

<u>**SECOND PART – VARIOUS TYPES OF CONTRACTS**</u>

<u>**TITLE NINE – DIRECTIVES**</u>

CHAPTER I – General Provisions [Powers of Attorney - Federal Code]

Article 2554.- In all general powers of attorney for lawsuits and the collection of money, ***the power of attorney*** is granted with all the general and special abilities that, according to law, require a special clause, so that the conferees **[persons to whom the power of attorney is given]** understand ***these abilities*** without limitation.

In general powers of attorney to administer assets, ***the power of attorney*** is granted with this characteristic **[administrative power]**, so that the representative has every kind of administrative power.

In general powers of attorney to exercise acts of ***ownership and use***, ***the power of attorney*** is granted with this characteristic so that the representative has the same rights as an owner pertaining to the assets, and ***the power*** to carry out every type of action to protect ***the assets***.

When, in the three cases mentioned above, it is desired to limit the representative's abilities, ***the power of attorney*** must ***either*** be recorded ***with these*** limitations, or the powers must be special.

Notarios (civil law notaries) must ***quote*** this article in the declaration **[document]** of the powers that are granted.

CÓDIGO CIVIL DEL ESTADO DE JALISCO

LIBRO QUINTO – DE LAS DIVERSAS ESPECIES DE CONTRATOS

TÍTULO NOVENO – DEL MANDATO

CAPÍTULO I – Disposiciones Generales

Artículo 2197.- El mandato es un contrato por el cual una persona llamada mandante otorga a otra denominada mandatario, la facultad de realizar por el otorgante un acto jurídico. Cuando el mandato tenga efectos patrimoniales, deberá entenderse que su finalidad es, la de conservar ese patrimonio.

Artículo 2198.- El contrato de mandato se perfecciona con la aceptación del mandatario.

Artículo 2199.- El mandato que implica el ejercicio de una profesión se presume aceptado, en términos generales, cuando es conferido a persona que ofrece al público el ejercicio de su profesión y el mandatario no lo rehusa dentro de los tres días siguientes a su conocimiento.

Artículo 2200.- El mandatario, en sus relaciones con el mandante, no estará obligado a intervenir en actos para los cuales no tenga instrucciones del mandante, ni en aquéllos en los que se considere impedido.

CIVIL CODE OF THE STATE OF JALISCO

BOOK FIVE – VARIOUS TYPES OF CONTRACTS

TITLE NINE – DIRECTIVES [Powers Of Attorney]

CHAPTER I – General Provisions [Powers of Attorney - State Code]

Article 2197.- A ***power of attorney*** is a contract by which a person called a *mandante* (grantor) grants another person called a *mandatario* (representative) the authority to carry out a legal act for the grantor. When the power of attorney has patrimonial consequences **[affects an inheritable asset – such as property]**, it is understood that its purpose is to protect that asset.

Article 2198.- The power of attorney contract ***takes effect*** on its acceptance by the representative.

Article 2199.- A power of attorney that entails the practice of a profession is presumed accepted, in general terms, when it is granted to a person who offers the practice of their profession to the public **[such as a lawyer]**, and the representative does not refuse within three **[3]** days after their ***knowledge of this action***.

Article 2200.- The representative, in their relationship with the grantor, is not obligated to become involved in acts for which they do not have instructions from the grantor, nor in those for which they consider themselves to be incapable.

Artículo 2201.- Los terceros no podrán exigir al mandatario su representación sino cuando haya aceptado especialmente para el acto de que se trate. La aceptación puede ser expresa o tácita. Habrá aceptación tácita cuando el mandatario ejecute cualquier acto en el negocio ejercitando el mandato.

Artículo 2202.- Pueden ser objeto del mandato todos los actos lícitos para los que la ley no exige la intervención personal del interesado.

Artículo 2203.- El mandato es esencialmente oneroso. Solamente será gratuito cuando así se haya convenido expresamente.

Artículo 2204.- El mandato debe de formalizarse por escrito, y otorgarse:

I. En escritura pública:

a) Siempre que sea general;

b) Cuando se refiera a inmuebles o a derechos reales;

c) Cuando el negocio para el que se confiera, su importe sea superior al equivalente a 300 días de salario mínimo; y

d) Cuando en virtud de él haya de ejecutar el mandatario algún acto que conforme a la ley deba constar en escritura pública;

Article 2201.- Third parties cannot ask the representative to represent them **unless the representative** has specifically agreed to the act they **have discussed**. Acceptance can be expressed or implied. There is implied acceptance when the representative carries out any act in the business **of** exercising the power of attorney.

Article 2202.- All legal acts for which the law does not require the personal intervention of the interested party can be the subject of a power of attorney.

Article 2203.- A power of attorney is fundamentally onerous **[the representative has legal obligations and responsibilities that might outweigh the benefits of being a representative]**. *The representative* can only be exempt *from this if* a specific agreement has been reached.

Article 2204.- The power of attorney must be formalised in writing, and granted:

I. In a publicly registered document:

a) Provided that it is general;

b) When it refers to real estate or real rights **[legal relationship between a person and one or more physical objects]**;

c) When the total value of the matter for which it is granted exceeds the equivalent of 300 days of the minimum wage; and

d) When by virtue of having to carry out some act of representation that according to law must be recorded in a public document;

II. En escrito privado, ante dos testigos y ratificadas las firmas del otorgante ante el notario público o servidor público que corresponda conocer del negocio para el que se otorga; y

III. En escrito privado sin ratificación de firmas en los demás casos.

Artículo 2205.- El mandato puede ser general o especial.

Artículo 2206.- Son mandatos generales:

I. Poder Judicial;

II. Poder para administrar bienes; y

III. Poder para ejercer actos de dominio.

Artículo 2207.-En los poderes generales judiciales, bastará decir que se otorgan con ese carácter, para que el apoderado pueda representar al poderdante en todo negocio de jurisdicción voluntaria, mixta y contenciosa, desde su principio hasta su fin; siempre que no se trate de actos que conforme a las leyes requieran poder especial, en tal caso se consignarán detalladamente las facultades que se confieran con su carácter de especialidad.

II. In a private document, in the presence of two witnesses, and the signature of the grantor is verified before a *notario público* (civil law notary) or a public servant that is expected to know about the matter *for which representation is* being granted; and

III. In other cases, in a private document without verification of the signatures *by a notario* [this could apply to condo assembly proxy forms].

Article 2205.- A power of attorney can be general or special.

Article 2206.- *The following* are general powers of attorney:

I. a power of attorney *giving your representative the authority to do anything financial, administrative, or legal in your name*;

II. Authority to administer assets; and

III. Authority to carry out acts *relating to* control and ownership [of property].

Article 2207.- For general powers of attorney, *the power of attorney* must be granted with this characteristic [a general power of attorney], so that the representative can act on behalf of the grantor in all matters of a voluntary jurisdiction [requiring no legal proceeding], contentious jurisdiction [matters in controversy between parties in a legal proceeding], and mixed, from its beginning to its end; provided that it does not deal with acts that require a special power of attorney according to law. In such a case, the *specific* rights that are conferred by the special power of attorney must be set out in detail.

Este tipo de poderes sólo podrá otorgarse a personas que tengan el título de abogado, licenciado en derecho o a quien no tenga ese carácter se encuentre asesorado necesariamente por profesionales del derecho, quien deberá suscribir y actuar conjuntamente con el apoderado, en todos los trámites judiciales.

En los poderes generales para administrar bienes, bastará decir que se otorgan con ese carácter, para que el apoderado tenga toda clase de facultades administrativas.

En los poderes generales para ejercer actos de dominio, será suficiente que se exprese que se confieren con ese carácter, a efecto de que el apoderado tenga todas las facultades de propietario, en lo relativo a los bienes como en su defensa.

Artículo 2208.- Cuando se quieran limitar las facultades del apoderado deberán consignarse expresa y claramente las limitaciones.

Artículo 2209.- Cuando el mandato no se otorgue en la forma prescrita en este título, el contrato será nulo y sólo quedarán subsistentes las obligaciones contraídas entre el tercero que haya procedido de buena fe y el mandatario, como si éste hubiese obrado en negocio propio.

*A **general** power **of attorney** can only be granted to people who have the title of *abogado* (lawyer), **are** a law graduate **[with a license certificate]**, or to **others** who obtain the necessary counsel of a legal professional; **this legal professional** must endorse and act together with the representative in all legal proceedings.

For general powers of attorney to administer assets, **the power of attorney** must be granted with this characteristic **[a general power of attorney to administer assets]**, so that the representative has every kind of administrative ability.

For general powers of attorney to carry out acts of **ownership and use**, **the power of attorney** must be granted with this characteristic **[a general power of attorney to carry out acts of ownership and use]**, with the effect that the representative has all of the abilities of an owner, relative to the assets in their protection.

Article 2208.- When **the grantor** wants to limit the representative's authority, the limitations must be expressly and clearly written.

Article 2209.- When the power of attorney is not granted in the manner prescribed in this title **[of the Code]**, the contract is invalid, and only the obligations agreed to between a third party who has acted in good faith and the representative will survive, as if **produced by a private transaction**.

Artículo 2210.- En el caso del artículo anterior, podrá el mandante exigir del mandatario la devolución de las sumas que le haya entregado, y respecto de las cuales será considerado el último como simple depositario.

Article 2210.- In the case of the previous article, the grantor can demand that the representative return any amounts *of money* that have been given to them *by the grantor*, and, in respect of which, this is considered to be the final *amount owed* like a simple *deposit held in trust*.

Artículo 2211.- Si el mandante, el mandatario y el que haya tratado con éste, proceden de mala fe, ninguno de ellos tendrá derecho a hacer valer la falta de forma del mandato.

Article 2211.- If the grantor, the representative, and *those who dealt with the business of the power of attorney* act in bad faith, none of them have the right to profit from a deficiency in the form of the power of attorney.

Artículo 2212.- El mandatario no es responsable para con los terceros con quienes contrata, sino cuando se obliga personalmente o traspasa los límites del mandato sin dar a aquéllos conocimiento suficiente de su poder.

Article 2212.- The representative is not responsible for third parties with whom they enter into a contract, except when *the representative* obligates themself personally, or goes beyond the limits of the power of attorney, without giving *the third parties* sufficient knowledge about *the representative's* authority.

Artículo 2213.- Cuando el mandatario obra en su propio nombre, el mandante no tiene acción contra las personas con quienes el mandatario ha contratado, ni éstas tampoco contra el mandante.

En este caso, el mandatario es el obligado directamente en favor de la persona con quien ha contratado, como si el asunto fuere personal suyo. Exceptúase el caso en que se trate de cosas propias del mandante.

Lo dispuesto en este artículo se entiende sin perjuicio de las acciones entre mandante y mandatario.

Article 2213.- When the representative acts in their own name, the grantor *cannot take* legal action against the people with which the representative has entered into a contract, *and vice versa*.

In this case, the representative is obligated directly to the person with whom they have entered a contract, as if the subject matter were their personal *business*. Except in the case where it deals with the grantor's property.

The provisions of this article are understood *to be* without detriment to the actions between the grantor and representative.

Artículo 2214.- Ningún poder se otorgará por una duración mayor a cinco años, salvo que antes de que se cumpla ese tiempo, el mandante lo revoque.

Article 2214.- No power of attorney can be granted for a duration longer than five [5] years, unless the grantor revokes it before that period is over.

Cuando durante la vigencia del poder, se hubiere iniciado un negocio cuya duración trascienda el término de su vigencia, se entenderán prorrogadas las facultades, hasta su conclusión, quedando comprendida la de intentar el juicio de Amparo.

Artículo 2215.- Para hacer factible la sustitución del apoderado en el contrato de mandato, deberá de señalarse en forma expresa dicha facultad.

Artículo 2216.- La sustitución de mandatario deberá hacerse con la misma formalidad con la cual se otorgó el mandato, señalándose expresamente el nombre del nuevo mandatario. Salvo el caso de que se trate de mandato otorgado en escritura pública, la sustitución, podrá hacerse constar en el primer testimonio.

When, during the valid term of a power *of attorney*, a proceeding is started that extends beyond the *power of attorney's* term of validity, it is understood that the date of the *power of attorney* is extended up to the conclusion *of the matter*, including the trying of an *Amparo* suit **[in México, this is a suit to stop the actions of a public authority while an appeal on constitutional grounds is undertaken against this authority – similar to an injunction]**.

Article 2215.- To be able to change the representative in the *power of attorney*, *this* ability must be written in a clear way *in the power of attorney document*.

Article 2216.- A change of representative must be carried out in the same *format in which the original power of attorney* was granted **[for example, a notarised document]**, setting out clearly the name of the new representative. Except in the case of a power of attorney granted by a publicly registered document, the change *of the representative* must be made evident in a *primer testimonio* (an original of a publicly registered document).

PART 9 – Legal Signatures & Electronic Transmissions

Civil Code of the State of Jalisco
Book Two – Title One
Articles 68 – 71, and
Book Four Part 1 – Title One
Articles 1261 & 1308,
&
Code of Civil Procedures of the State of Jalisco
Title Six
Article 298

Relevance to a Condominium

Many documents used by a condo need legal signatures. These include contracts, including powers of attorney and proxies.

It's important to know what's needed to make a signed document legal. **Articles 68 through 71** of the Civil Code define what is acceptable as a legal signature.

Before any contract can exist, there must be a willingness by the parties to accept the conditions of the contract. **Article 1261** of the Civil Code defines how this willingness can be expressed, including by means of technology.

Contracts that don't require the use of a *notario* (civil law notary), such as a proxy, have more relaxed rules for signatures. **Article 1308** of the Civil Code governs the acceptance of signed documents transmitted by electronic means.

It's important to know whether faxes or emails can be used as evidence in a lawsuit. **Article 298** of the Code of Civil Procedures lists the accepted documentary evidence.

Versions of Laws Used

Codes and laws are living documents that are amended frequently by the level of government that issued them.

This section contains excerpts from:

> the *Código Civil del Estado de Jalisco* (Civil Code of the State of Jalisco), that took effect on **September 14, 1995**, and was last amended on *December 20, 2014*; and

> the *Código de Procedimientos Civiles del Estado de Jalisco* (Code of Civil Procedures of the State of Jalisco), that took effect on **January 1, 1939**, and was last amended on *November 29, 2014*.

Sections of the Laws Used

The excerpts from the **Jalisco Civil Code** translated in this section are from: *Libro Segundo – Título Primero*

Libro Segundo (Book Two) is titled *"De las personas y de las instituciones de familia"* (Persons and Family Entities);

Título Primero (Title One) is titled *"De las personas físicas"* (Individuals);

and *Libro Cuatro Primera Parte – Título Primero*:

Libro Cuarto Primera Parte (Book Four Part One) is titled *"De las obligaciones en general"* (Obligations in General).

Título Primero (Title One) is titled *"Fuentes de las obligaciones"* (Sources of Obligations).

The excerpt from the **Jalisco Code of Civil Procedures** translated in this section is from *Título Sexto*:

Título Sexto (Title Six) is titled *"Del Juicio Ordinario"* (The Ordinary Lawsuit).

CÓDIGO CIVIL DEL ESTADO DE JALISCO	CIVIL CODE OF THE STATE OF JALISCO

CÓDIGO CIVIL DEL ESTADO DE JALISCO

LIBRO SEGUNDO

TÍTULO PRIMERO – DE LAS PERSONAS FÍSICAS

CAPÍTULO IX – De la Individualización de las Personas Físicas

Artículo 68.- Firma es la expresión gráfica que estampa una persona para dejar constancia de su voluntad en el documento que con su persona está referido.

Esta expresión gráfica es libre y solamente se tendrá como auténtica, para efectos de cotejo y comprobación, aquélla que se estampe en presencia de servidores públicos o con motivo de funciones oficiales.

Artículo 69.- La manuscripción y el estampar dos huellas digitales constituye conjunta o separadamente otras formas de identificar a sus autores por medio de los métodos científicos.

Artículo 70.- En todos los actos jurídicos en que intervenga una persona y que tenga el carácter de solemne y en los que la ley así lo exija, deberán ser firmados, manuscrito el nombre y estampar dos huellas digitales de sus suscriptores y otorgantes.

Artículo 71.- La persona que no sepa o no pueda firmar ni escribir, estampará cuando menos como medio de identificación sus huellas digitales, debiendo hacerlo ante dos testigos o ante servidor público.

CIVIL CODE OF THE STATE OF JALISCO

BOOK TWO

TITLE ONE – INDIVIDUALS

CHAPTER IX – Characteristics of the Individual

Article 68.- A signature is a graphical representation imprinted by a person to leave a record of their intent in a document in which their *identity* is referenced.

This graphical representation is self-contained, and can only be considered authentic for effects of comparison and verification when *made* in the presence of public officials, or because of official acts.

Article 69.- A mark **[a symbol such as an 'X' or a printed name]** plus the stamping of two fingerprints, constitutes jointly or separately other ways of identifying the *signor* by means of scientific methods.

Article 70. In every legal proceeding in which a person becomes involved, and *in which* they have a formal role, and in which the law demands it, *the documents* must be signed, the name printed out, and stamped *with* two fingerprints of their endorsers and signatories.

Article 71. A person who does not know how to, or cannot, sign or write, must stamp, at least as a means of identification, their fingerprints, which must be made in front of two witnesses or in front of a public official.

<u>CÓDIGO CIVIL DEL ESTADO DE JALISCO</u>

<u>LIBRO CUATRO</u>

<u>TÍTULO PRIMERO – FUENTES DE LAS OBLIGACIONES</u>

CAPÍTULO I – Disposiciones generales

Artículo 1261.- La voluntad, como fuente de obligaciones, puede ser expresa o tácita; debiendo presumirse cuando una persona ejecuta actos o acepta beneficios que no se pueden explicar, dentro de la equidad y la justicia, sin el reconocimiento de las obligaciones correlativas, para ello se estará a lo siguiente:

I. Será expresa cuando se manifiesta verbalmente, por escrito, por medios electrónicos, ópticos o de cualquier otra tecnología o por signos inequívocos; y

II. Será tácita cuando resulte de hechos o de actos que la presupongan o que autoricen a presumirlo, excepto en los casos en que por ley o por convenio deba manifestarse expresamente.

<u>CIVIL CODE OF THE STATE OF JALISCO</u>

<u>BOOK FOUR</u>

<u>TITLE ONE – SOURCES OF OBLIGATIONS</u>

CHAPTER I – General Provisions [Sources of Obligations]

Article 1261.- Willingness, as the source of obligations **[a contract]**, can be *either* express or tacit; *willingness* must be presumed when a person carries out acts or accepts benefits that cannot be explained, using fairness and justice, *as being* without an acknowledgement of the corresponding obligations; for this *to occur* the following must exist:

I. *Willingness* is express when it is declared verbally, in writing, by electronic media, optical media, by any other technology, or by unequivocal indications; and

II. *Willingness* is tacit when it results from actions or acts that presuppose it, or that permit the presumption of it, except in cases in which, by law or by agreement, it must be declared explicitly.

CAPÍTULO II – De los contratos

Artículo 1308.- Cuando se exija la forma escrita para el contrato, los documentos relativos deben ser firmados por todas las personas que en el acto deban intervenir, salvo lo que previene este código para las personas que no saben o no pueden firmar.

Lo previsto por el párrafo que antecede se tendrá por cumplido mediante la utilización de medios electrónicos, ópticos, firma electrónica o de cualquier otra tecnología en los términos de la Ley estatal aplicable, siempre y cuando la información generada o comunicada en forma íntegra, a través de dichos medios, sea atribuible a las personas obligadas, pueda existir permanentemente y sea accesible para su ulterior consulta.

CHAPTER II – Contracts

Article 1308.- When a contract **[proxies and powers of attorney are both contracts]** is called for in written form, the corresponding documents must be signed by everyone involved in the act *covered by the contract*, except *as previously described in* this Code for people that do not know how to, or cannot, sign their names.

The preceding paragraph **[signing of a contract]** is considered to have been fulfilled by the use of electronic media **[defined under Jalisco law as: *"technology devices used to transmit or store data and information, through computers, telephone lines, dedicated links, microwaves. or of any other technology"*]**, optical media, electronic signature **[using a digital certificate]**, or any other technology, under the terms of the applicable state law, if and when the information generated or communicated by this means is in its entirety **[the entire document – cannot be a portion of it]**, can be attributed to the contracted persons, exists permanently, and is accessible for further examination **[the transmitted documents must be kept in the records, and must not be destroyed]**.

En los casos en que la **Ley establezca como requisito que un acto jurídico deba otorgarse en instrumento ante fedatario público, éste y las partes obligadas podrán generar, enviar, recibir, archivar o comunicar la información que contenga los términos exactos en que las partes han decidido obligarse, mediante la utilización de firma electrónica en los términos de la Ley estatal aplicable, en cuyo caso el fedatario público, deberá hacer constar en el propio instrumento los elementos a través** de los cuales se atribuye dicha información a las partes y conservar bajo su resguardo una versión íntegra de la misma para su ulterior consulta, otorgando dicho instrumento de conformidad con la legislación aplicable que lo rige.

In those cases in which the law establishes the requirement that a legal act must be granted as a legal instrument before a ***public notary***, ***the notario*** and the parties obligated ***by the act*** can generate, send, receive, file, or communicate the information containing the exact terms to which the parties have agreed to obligate themselves, by means of the use of an electronic signature under the terms of the applicable state law [***Ley de Firma Electrónica Avanzada para el Estado de Jalisco* – this paragraph refers to electronic signatures generated by a digital certificate authority, and not to a simple email or fax**], in which case the ***public notary*** must make evident in their ***document*** the factors by which said information is attributed to the parties, keeping under their protection an unabridged version of the same for subsequent examination [**in the *notario's* protocol book**], issuing the aforementioned document in accordance with the applicable legislation that governs it.

CÓDIGO DE PROCEDIMIENTOS CIVILES DEL ESTADO DE JALISCO	CODE OF CIVIL PROCEDURES OF THE STATE OF JALISCO

TÍTULO SEXTO – DEL JUICIO ORDINARIO

TITLE SIX – THE ORDINARY LAWSUIT

CAPÍTULO II – Reglas Generales de la Prueba

CHAPTER II – General Rules of Evidence

Artículo 298.- La ley reconoce como medios de prueba:

Article 298.- The law recognises as instruments of evidence *the following*:

I. Confesión;

I. a confession;

II. Documentos públicos;

II. public documents **[registered at the public registry]**;

III. Documentos privados;

III. private documents;

IV. Dictámenes periciales;

IV. expert testimony;

V. Reconocimiento o inspección judicial;

V. judicial acknowledgement or inspection;

VI. Declaraciones de testigos;

VI. witness statements;

VII. Fotografías, copias fotostáticas, registros dactiloscópicos, y, en general, todos aquellos elementos aportados por los descubrimientos de la ciencia;

VII. photographs, photocopies, fingerprint records, and, in general, all those elements submitted by scientific discoveries **[forensic evidence]**;

VIII. La declaración de parte;

VIII. declarations by the parties;

IX. Presunciones;

IX. legal presumptions **[the existence of an assumed fact derived from the proof of other facts by other evidence]**;

X. Información generada o comunicada que conste en medios electrónicos, ópticos o en cualquier otra tecnología; y

X. information generated or communicated that is presented by electronic media, optical media, or by any other technology; and

XI. Los demás medios que produzcan convicción en el juzgador.

XI. other means that produce certainty in the judge **[in the Judge's opinion]**.

Siempre que las partes ofrezcan cualquier otro medio de prueba distinto de los nominados expresamente en este Código, el juez, al admitirlo, se sujetará a las reglas generales establecidas en este capítulo y a las particulares a que más se asemeje.

When the parties offer any other instrument of evidence that differs from those named specifically in this Code, the judge, to be able to admit it, will abide by the general rules established in this chapter, and to the matters to which they are most similar.

PART 10 – Civil Associations

Civil Code of the State of Jalisco
Book 2 – Title 3
Articles 172 – 189

Relevance to Condominiums

Condominiums in Jalisco, unlike their counterparts in Canada and the U.S., are no longer administered by a condo owners' association. However, most older condominiums (incorporated before 1995), and all *fraccionamientos* (fraccs), are administered by an association.

Condominiums established after 1995 are incorporated into a *régimen de Condominio* (condominium regime) under the Civil Code. This regime contains all the elements of a condo owners' association, but is not an association. Before 1995, the condo regime was regulated by a separate condo law (outside of the Civil Code).

Further, since 1995, the condominium regime became a separate legal entity under state law (see *Part 6 – Legal Entities* for more information on this concept), with full legal rights to act on behalf of the titleholders of the property within the condo. The abilities of this legal entity are fully described in **Book Three – Title Six** of the Jalisco Civil Code (the full translation of this is in this book: see *Part 3 – The Jalisco Condo Law*). Before 1995, this was not the case, and a civil association was needed to legally represent the condo regime.

Condos established before 1995 are still regulated by whatever condo law was in effect at the time the condo was set up, unless, sometime after 1995, the condo regime was re-established under the new law.

One of the main reasons the condominium legislation was moved to the Civil Code, and a separate legal entity created, was to eliminate many of the problems associated with administration by an association. For example, membership in an association in Jalisco cannot be made mandatory, and, therefore, members can opt-out and, because of this, avoid the obligation to pay fees.

The *Asociación Civil* (Civil Association) or *A.C.* is a separate legal entity from a condo regime, and it is regulated by a different section of the Civil Code.

It's important to understand that an association and a condo regime are two separate and different legal entities, and are governed by separate and different laws.

This section of the book contains a translation of the part of the Code that regulates associations. It's much less specific than the code section that controls condominium regimes (since associations can be set up for a wide variety of purposes), and any given association is largely controlled by its statutes (by-laws) – provided they don't contradict the main law on associations.

Version of Laws Used

Codes and laws are living documents that are amended frequently by the level of government that issued them.

This section contains an excerpt from the *Código Civil del Estado de Jalisco* (Civil Code of the State of Jalisco), that took effect on **September 14, 1995**, and was last amended on ***December 20, 2014.***

Sections of the Laws Used

The excerpt from the **Jalisco Civil Code** translated in this section is *Libro Segundo – Título Tercero*:

Libro Segundo (Book Two) is titled *"De las personas y de las instituciones de familia"* (Persons and Family Entities).

Título Tercero (Title Three) is titled *"De las personas jurídicas"* (Legal Entities).

| CÓDIGO CIVIL DEL ESTADO DE JALISCO | CIVIL CODE OF THE STATE OF JALISCO |

CÓDIGO CIVIL DEL ESTADO DE JALISCO

LIBRO SEGUNDO

TÍTULO TERCERO – DE LAS PERSONAS JURIDICAS

CAPÍTULO II – De Las Asociaciones

Artículo 172.- Cuando varias personas convienen en reunirse, de manera que no sea enteramente transitoria, para realizar un fin común que no esté prohibido por la ley y que no tenga carácter preponderantemente económico, constituyen una asociación.

Artículo 173.- El acto jurídico por el que se constituya una asociación, debe constar en escritura pública otorgada ante notario, que tenga su adscripción en el domicilio de la asociación.

Tratándose de asociaciones que tengan como objeto aspectos relacionado (sic) con la asistencia social, deberá contar con la anuencia por escrito del Instituto Jalisciense de Asistencia Social, misma que tendrá que presentarse ante el notario previo a su constitución.

Artículo 174.- El testimonio que expida el notario, deberá ser inscrito en el Registro Público de la Propiedad que corresponda al domicilio de la asociación y desde ese momento tiene personalidad jurídica propia.

CIVIL CODE OF THE STATE OF JALISCO

BOOK TWO

TITLE THREE – LEGAL ENTITIES

CHAPTER II – Associations

Article 172.- When several people agree to come together, in a way that is not entirely temporary, to carry out a common goal that is not forbidden by law, and that does not have a primarily economic purpose, they can establish an association **[for economic purposes, a society is the correct choice]**.

Article 173.- The legal act by which an association is established must be recorded in a publicly registered document executed before a *notario* (civil law notary) who has been assigned to practice in the **place where the association is located**.

Associations whose objective is related to social assistance, must have the written approval of the *Instituto Jalisciense de Asistencia Social* (Jalisco Institute of Social Assistance), which they must present to the *notario* before their formation **as an association**.

Article 174.- The sworn declaration that the *notario* issues must be registered in the *Registro Público de la Propiedad* (Public Registry of Property) that corresponds to **the place where the association is located**, and, from that moment, **the association** has its own legal capacity **[it becomes a legal person or entity]**.

Artículo 175.- Si la asociación no consta en escritura pública, o no se ha inscrito en el Registro Público de la Propiedad y se adquieren por los integrantes de los órganos de administración o representación obligaciones frente a terceros, la asociación será considerada como irregular, quedando obligados en forma solidaria quienes a nombre de la misma hubieren contratado.

Artículo 176.- La falta de registro, da derecho a cualesquiera de los integrantes de la asociación a reclamar, bien sea su disolución o su regularización, por medio de la inscripción en el Registro Público de la Propiedad.

Artículo 177.- Las asociaciones serán representadas por un director general o por un consejo de directores o las denominaciones que señalen los estatutos quienes tendrán las facultades que se les confieran en los mismos.

Artículo 178.- Cuando se nombre consejo de directores u órgano equivalente, el número de los mismos deberá ser impar. En todo caso, el presidente del consejo tendrá voto de calidad para la toma de decisiones.

Artículo 179.- Cuando por cualquier causa no haya director nombrado, o habiéndolo se hubiere ausentado del domicilio de la asociación, quien tenga interés en que se haga la designación, podrá solicitar al juez que tenga jurisdicción en el domicilio de la asociación, que convoque a asamblea para realizar el nombramiento respectivo; en caso de suma urgencia, el juez podrá hacerla subsistiendo la designación hasta en tanto no sea hecha por los asociados.

Article 175.- If the association is not recorded in a public document, or *if* it has not been registered in the *Registro Público de la Propiedad*, and *the association* acquires obligations *to* third parties by the members of its administrative or representative bodies, the association is considered as nonconforming, and *the people* who entered into the contract in the name of *the association* will be jointly responsible **[personally]**.

Article 176.- A lack of *public* registration gives any member of the association *the* right to sue for *either the association's* dissolution or normalisation **[making the association legal]** by means of registration in the *Registro Público de la Propiedad*.

Article 177.- Associations must be represented by a General Director, a board of directors, or by the bodies named in their statutes. *These* will have the authority granted to them by *the statutes*.

Article 178.- When a Board of Directors or similar body is appointed, it must have an odd number *of members*. In any case, the President **[or Chair]** of the Board has *the tie-breaking vote* for decisions.

Article 179.- When, for any reason, there is no appointed *General Director*, or an existing one has left the association, those who are interested in being appointed *to that position*, can ask a judge who has jurisdiction in *the location of* the association *to* convene an assembly to carry out this appointment. In cases of utmost urgency, a judge can make an appointment, even if it is not made by the members of the association.

Artículo 180.- La asamblea general se reunirá en la época fijada en los estatutos o cuando sea convocada por la dirección. Esta deberá citar a asamblea cuando para ello fuere requerida por lo menos por el cinco por ciento de los asociados, o si no lo hiciere, en su lugar lo hará el juez de lo civil a petición de dichos asociados.

Article 180.- The general assembly must meet in the period of time set out in the statutes, or when convened by the administration *of the association*. *The administration* must call a meeting when *it is* wanted by at least five percent **[5%]** of the members of the association, or if *they do not*, *one will be held* in a place *designated* by a judge of the civil court at the request of the aforementioned members.

Artículo 181.- La asamblea general resolverá:

I. Sobre la admisión y exclusión de asociados;

II. Sobre la disolución anticipada de la asociación o sobre su prórroga por más tiempo del fijado en los estatutos;

III. Sobre el nombramiento de director o directores cuando no hayan sido nombrados en la escritura constitutiva;

IV. Sobre la revocación de los nombramientos hechos; y

V. Sobre los demás asuntos que le encomienden los estatutos.

Article 181.- The general assembly decides on:

I. the admission and exclusion of members;

II. the anticipated dissolution of the association, or *on* its extension for a duration longer than that which was set out in its statutes;

III. the appointment of a *General Director* or *board of directors* when they have not been appointed in the establishing public document **[the articles of association]**.

IV. the revocation of appointments *already* made; and

V. all other items authorised by the statutes.

Artículo 182.- Los acuerdos tomados en las asambleas generales son obligatorios para todos los asociados, aun cuando se hubiere votado en contra de los mismos.

Article 182.- The agreements *reached* in the general assemblies are binding *on* all members of the association, even when they voted against *these resolutions*.

El asociado que reclame la irregularidad en la citación o notificación para concurrir a la asamblea, o que ésta se hubiere ocupado de asuntos no contenidos en la convocatoria, podrá reclamar ante el juez del domicilio de la asociación, la inaplicabilidad a su persona de los acuerdos tomados en la misma.

La resolución que en éste caso se dicte sólo afectará a quien lo promovió; pero cuando se hubiere convenido sobre la constitución de gravamen o enajenación de los activos fijos de la asociación, de su disolución anticipada, de su fusión con otras asociaciones o de su escisión, podrá demandarse la nulidad de dichos acuerdos.

Quien reclame la nulidad de los acuerdos de una asamblea, podrá pedir al juez que de manera provisional ordene la suspensión de los mismos, siempre que se otorgue por el demandante garantía suficiente para responder por los daños y perjuicios que se causen por tal medida, si es que no tiene la resolución favorable a sus pretensiones. La garantía señalada podrá aumentarse o disminuirse si varían las condiciones que se tomaron en consideración para fijarla.

Artículo 183.- Cada asociado gozará de un voto en las asambleas generales.

Artículo 184.- Los miembros de la asociación tendrán derecho de separarse de ella, previo aviso dado con dos meses de anticipación.

A member that claims an irregularity in the call or notice to attend the assembly, or that items were taken up at the assembly that were not contained in the call, can file a suit with a judge in the location of the association to make the agreements reached in *the assembly* inapplicable to them **[the person filing the suit]**.

The decision in this case only applies to the person who brought the suit. However, when *the association* makes an agreement about the creation of a lien, the sale of the fixed assets of the association, its merger with another association, or its dissolution, *the person filing this suit* can sue for the nullification of such an agreement.

Whoever files a suit to nullify the agreements of an assembly, can ask a judge to order the temporary suspension of *these agreements*, provided that the complainant provides a guaranty **[bond]** sufficient to *cover* the damages or losses that *could be* caused by such action if a favourable decision is not *handed down by the judge*. *This* guaranty can be increased or decreased *in value* if the conditions that were taken into consideration when securing *the bond* change.

Article 183.- Each member of the association has the right to one vote in the general assemblies.

Article 184.- The members of the association have the right *to leave the association* **[give up their membership]** by giving two months advance notice.

Artículo 185.- Los asociados sólo podrán ser excluidos de la asociación, por las causas que señalen los estatutos, según acuerdo de la asamblea general en la que deberán ser oídos.

Article 185.- The members of an association can only be removed from the association for causes set out in the statutes, **and** pursuant to an agreement of the general assembly in which they **[the member to be expelled]** must be heard.

Artículo 186.- Los asociados tienen derecho de vigilar que las cuotas se dediquen al fin que se propone la asociación y con ese objeto, pueden examinar los libros de contabilidad y demás papeles de ésta.

Article 186.- The members of the association have the right to **make sure** that the membership dues are dedicated to the ends intended by the association, and, **for** that purpose, can examine the account books and other papers of **the association**.

Artículo 187.- La calidad de asociado es intransferible.

Article 187.- **Membership in an association** is not transferable.

Artículo 188.- Las asociaciones, además de las causas previstas en los estatutos, se extinguen:

Article 188.- Associations, in addition to the causes **set out** in the statutes, **can be terminated by the following**:

I. Por consentimiento de la asamblea general;

I. By agreement of the general assembly;

II. Por haber concluido el término fijado para su duración o por haber conseguido totalmente el objeto de su constitución;

II. By having finished the term set out for its life, or by having fully achieved the purpose of its formation;

III. Por haberse vuelto incapaces de realizar el fin para que fueron constituidas; y

III. By having **become** incapable of fulfilling the **purpose** for which it was formed; and

IV. Por resolución dictada por autoridad competente.

IV.- By a decision imposed by a competent authority **[such as a court]**.

Artículo 189.- En caso de disolución, los bienes de la asociación se aplicarán conforme a lo que determinen los estatutos y a falta de disposición de estos, según lo que determine la asamblea general.

Article 189.- In case of dissolution **of the association**, the assets of the association must be **dealt with** according to the statutes **of the association** and, when there is a lack of instructions **in the statutes**, pursuant to the decisions of the general assembly.

PART 11 – Limitations on Collecting Debts

Civil Code of the State of Jalisco
Book 4 Part 1 – Title 5
Articles 1732 – 1748

Relevance to a Condominium

It's important to know that collection of delinquent fees is limited to two years from their due date by **Article 1743** of the Civil Code.

The accumulation of time to count against this limit stops on the date you file a lawsuit.

This means that if you wait too long to start a suit against a delinquent owner, you can't collect older debts through the courts. As you wait longer to start legal proceedings after this two year limit has run out, more of this early debt will "fall off," and become uncollectable.

This time period is calculated from the date of your court filing, and goes back two years to encompass all fees and charges that had payment dates falling in this two year period.

It's important to know that the "due date" for collections of condo fees is 90 days **after** the due date for payment (see **Article 1029** in *Part 3 – The Jalisco Condo Law*). Therefore, you have two years plus 90 days from the court filing date back to the earliest date on which payment was requested. See our companion book, the *"Jalisco Condo Manual – Second Edition"* for condo debt collection procedures.

Versions of Laws Used

Codes and laws are living documents that are amended frequently by the level of government that issued them.

This section contains an excerpt from the *Código Civil del Estado de Jalisco* (Civil Code of the State of Jalisco), that took effect on **September 14, 1995**, and was last amended on *December 20, 2014.*

Sections of the Laws Used

The excerpt from the **Jalisco Civil Code** translated in this section is from: *Libro Cuatro Primera Parte – Título Quinto*:

Libro Cuarto Primera Parte (Book Four Part One) is titled *"De las obligaciones en general"* (Obligations in General).

Título Quinto (Title Five) is titled *"Extinción de las obligaciones"* (Termination of Obligations).

Definitions

This entire section is based on a specific legal term:

<u>prescription</u>: a legal process letting a court remove a debtor's obligation after a specified period of time.

This is a protection mechanism in favour of the **debtor** (person who owes the debt), and against a **creditor** (person to whom the debt is owed).

This could happen, for example, if a condo tried to sue a delinquent owner for unpaid fees going back more than two years plus 90 days. The defence lawyer would claim prescription, and the entire lawsuit could be dismissed.

For clarity, I have replaced the word "*prescription*" with the term "***Debt Cancellation***" in the translated text.

CÓDIGO CIVIL DEL ESTADO DE JALISCO	CIVIL CODE OF THE STATE OF JALISCO

LIBRO CUATRO PRIMERA PARTE

BOOK FOUR PART ONE

TÍTULO QUINTO – EXTINCIÓN DE LAS OBLIGACIONES

TITLE FIVE – TERMINATION OF OBLIGATIONS

CAPÍTULO V – Prescripción

CHAPTER V – Prescription
[a legal process letting a court remove a debtor's obligation after a specified period of time – referred to as Debt Cancellation in this text for clarity]

Artículo 1732.- Prescripción es un medio de librarse de obligaciones mediante el transcurso de cierto tiempo, por no exigirse su cumplimiento.

Article 1732.- Prescription **[debt cancellation after time]** is a means for disposing of obligations because of the passage of a given time period, by not requiring the fulfilment *of these obligations*.

Artículo 1733.- La prescripción aprovecha a todos, aún a los que por sí mismos no pueden obligarse, debe ser reclamada ya que no opera oficiosamente.

Article 1733.- *Debt Cancellation* is available to all *debtors*, however, it should be claimed for those who cannot act for themselves, since it does not come about unofficially **[without an action being taken]**.

Artículo 1734.- Las personas con capacidad para enajenar pueden renunciar a la prescripción ganada, pero no el derecho de prescribir para lo sucesivo.

Article 1734.- People with the capability of transferring ownership can waive an awarded *Debt Cancellation*, but not the right of future *Debt Cancellations for the goods or property*.

Artículo 1735.- La renuncia de la prescripción es expresa o tácita, siendo esta última la que resulta de un hecho que importa el reconocimiento de la subsistencia de la obligación.

Article 1735.- A waiver of a *Debt Cancellation* is *either* express or implicit, this last **[implicit waiver]** results from any act that signifies an admission of the continued existence of the obligation **[on the part of the debtor]**.

Artículo 1736.- La prescripción adquirida por el deudor principal aprovecha a los deudores solidarios y a los fiadores.

Article 1736.- A *Debt Cancellation* obtained by the principal debtor *is also available to* joint debtors and to guarantors.

Artículo 1737.- La excepción que por prescripción adquiera un codeudor solidario, no aprovechará a los demás sino cuando el tiempo exigido haya debido correr del mismo modo para todos ellos.

Article 1737.- The exception is that if a jointly responsible debtor is acquired through *the Debt Cancellation process*, the other *debtors* cannot benefit from the *Debt Cancellation until* the prescribed time period has *expired* in the same way for all of *the debtors*.

Artículo 1738.- En el caso previsto por el Artículo que precede, el acreedor sólo podrá exigir a los deudores que no prescribieren, el valor de la obligación deducida la parte que corresponde al deudor que prescribió.

Article 1738.- In the case mentioned in the preceding article, a creditor can only demand from debtors that have not *exercised Debt Cancellation*, the value of the obligation minus the part that corresponds to the debtors that have *exercised Debt Cancellation*.

Artículo 1739.- El Estado, los municipios y las demás personas jurídicas de orden público se considerarán como particulares para la prescripción de las acciones y los derechos de orden privado que tengan a su favor o en su contra.

Article 1739.- The State, the municipalities, and other *public institutions* are considered as private individuals for the *purposes of Debt Cancellation* of actions and private rights of demand **[rights that exist between individuals, rather than public rights which exist between individuals and governments]** that *these public bodies* have *either* in their favour or against them.

Artículo 1740.- Fuera de los casos expresamente exceptuados por la ley, se necesita el lapso de cinco años, contando desde que una obligación pudo exigirse, para que prescriba el derecho de pedir su cumplimiento.

Article 1740.- Except for cases specifically exempted by the law, an elapsed time of five [5] years, counted from the time when an obligation can be demanded **[is legally due]**, is required so that the right of asking for its fulfilment can be *legally cancelled*.

Artículo 1741.- La obligación de dar alimentos es imprescriptible.

Article 1741.- The obligation to provide support **[to family members]** cannot be *legally cancelled*.

Artículo 1742.- Prescriben en dos años:

I. Los honorarios profesionales u otras retribuciones por la prestación de cualquier servicio. La prescripción comienza a correr desde la fecha en que dejaron de prestarse los servicios;

II. La acción de los hoteleros para cobrar el importe del hospedaje, y la de éstos y la de los fonderos para cobrar el precio de los alimentos que ministren. La prescripción corre desde el día en que debió ser pagado el hospedaje, o desde aquél en que se ministraron los alimentos; y

III. La responsabilidad civil proveniente de hechos ilícitos que no constituyan delitos. La prescripción corre desde el día en que se verificaron los mismos.

Artículo 1743.- Las pensiones, rentas, alquileres, pago de intereses y cualesquiera otras prestaciones periódicas no cobradas a su vencimiento, quedarán prescritas en dos años contados, escalonadamente, desde el vencimiento de cada una de ellas, ya se haga el cobro en virtud de acción real o de acción personal.

Artículo 1744.- Prescribe en dos años la obligación de rendir cuentas. En igual término prescriben las obligaciones líquidas que resulten de la rendición de cuentas. En el primer caso, la prescripción comienza a correr desde el día en que el obligado termina su administración; en el segundo caso, desde el día en que la liquidación es aprobada por los interesados.

Article 1742.- The following can be ***legally cancelled after*** two **[2]** years:

I. Professional fees or other payments for the rendering of any service. The ***Debt Cancellation time period*** begins from the date on which the rendering of services stopped;

II. The act of hoteliers billing the value of rooms, furnishing lodging, and for innkeepers to charge the price of meals they provide. The ***Debt Cancellation time period*** is from the day on which the hotel should have been paid, or from the day on which they provided the meals; and

III. The civil responsibility originating from illicit acts that do not constitute crimes. The ***Debt Cancellation time period*** starts from the day on which ***these acts*** were verified as such.

Article 1743.- Pensions, private income, rent, interest payments, and any other periodic contributions **[such as condo fees]** not collected by their due date, can be ***legally cancelled*** in two years, counted sequentially from the due date of each of ***periodic contribution***. At the end of the two years, the ability to collect payment is ended either through real or personal action.

Article 1744.- The obligation to render accounts can be ***legally cancelled*** after two years. In an equal term, the net liabilities **[debt]** that result from the rendering of accounts can be ***legally cancelled***. In the first case, the ***Debt Cancellation time period*** starts from the day on which the debtor finished their administration ***of the account***. In the second case, from the day on which the liquidation ***of the account*** is approved by those concerned.

Artículo 1745.- La prescripción se suspende y, por tanto, no puede comenzar ni correr:

I. Entre ascendientes y descendientes, durante la patria potestad;

II. Entre los incapacitados y sus tutores mientras dura la tutela;

III. Entre consortes mientras subsista legalmente su unión matrimonial;

IV. Entre personas que no estando casados y sin que haya impedimento no dispensable para contraer matrimonio entre ellas, viven como si lo estuvieren, mientras dure el estado aparente matrimonial;

V. Entre copropietarios o coposeedores, respecto del bien común;

VI. Entre los coherederos por los derechos que entre sí y con relación a la herencia tengan que reclamarse, mientras no se haga la partición definitiva;

VII. Entre las personas cuyos bienes estén sometidos por la ley o por providencia del juez a la administración de otros y éstos, respecto de los actos y responsabilidades inherentes a la administración, mientras no se haya presentado y aprobado definitivamente la cuenta;

VIII. Entre las personas jurídicas y sus administradores mientras éstos estén en el cargo, por las acciones de responsabilidad contra ellos;

Article 1745.- *Debt Cancellation* is suspended and, therefore, cannot begin or operate:

I. Between parents and children, during parental custody **[while children live at home]**;

II. Between the incapacitated and their guardians, while the guardianship persists;

III. Between a married couple, while their matrimonial union legally exists;

IV. Between people who are not married to each other, are living as if they were in *a marriage*, and while this apparent matrimonial state continues without there being a nonremovable impediment to contract marriage between them;

V. Between co-owners or joint possessors, regarding their common property;

VI. Between joint heirs, for the rights that they have with each other regarding the inheritance they have a claim to, but who have not made a definite division;

VII. Between persons regarding the acts and inherent responsibilities of the administration of their goods which have been subjugated by the law, or by order of a judge, to the administration of others, while they have not appeared in person and specifically approved the account;

VIII. Between enterprises and their administrators, for actions of responsibility against *these administrators*, while they are in their position **[job]**;

IX. Entre el deudor que ha ocultado dolosamente la existencia de la deuda y el acreedor, mientras el dolo no haya sido descubierto;

X. Para los menores y mayores incapacitados mientras no tengan representante legal en forma individualizada, y por seis meses más siguientes al nombramiento del mismo, o a la cesación de la incapacidad;

XI. Para quienes se encuentran en servicio público fuera del territorio del Estado; y

XII. Para los militares en servicio activo y civiles al servicio de las fuerzas armadas, en tiempo de guerra, tanto fuera como dentro del Estado.

Artículo 1746.- La prescripción se interrumpe:

I. Por la presentación de la demanda aunque la misma no hubiere sido notificada o por cualquier género de requerimiento o de interpelación hecha al deudor. Se considerará la prescripción como no interrumpida si el actor desistiese el requerimiento, de la interpelación o de la demanda, o fuese ésta desestimada, u operare la caducidad de la instancia; y

II. Porque la persona a cuyo favor transcurre la prescripción reconozca expresamente, de palabra o por escrito, o tácitamente por hechos indudables, el derecho de la persona contra quien prescribe.

IX. Between a debtor who has deceitfully concealed the existence of the debt and their creditor, while the bad act has not been discovered;

X. For minors and incapacitated adults while they do not have a specified legal representative, and for six months more following the designation of *a representative*, or the end of the incapacity;

XI. For those who are in public service outside of the State territory; and

XII. For the military in active service, and civilians in the service of the Armed Forces in wartime, whether outside or inside the State.

Article 1746.- *Debt Cancellation* is suspended:

I. By the launching of a lawsuit, even though *the suit* has not been served, for any type of summons, or an appeal made by the debtor. A *Debt Cancellation* is considered as not interrupted if the plaintiff gives up the summons, the appeal, or the lawsuit, or *these are* dismissed, or the lapsing of a legal action occurs; and

II. Because the person, in whose favour the *Debt Cancellation* takes effect **[the debtor]**, acknowledges explicitly, verbally, or in writing, or implicitly by indisputable acts, the right of the person being prescribed against **[the creditor]**.

Empezará a contarse el nuevo término de la prescripción, en caso de reconocimiento de las obligaciones, desde el día en que se haga; si se renueva el documento, desde la fecha del nuevo título, y si se hubiere prorrogado el plazo del cumplimiento de la obligación, desde el vencimiento del nuevo plazo o prórroga.

Artículo 1747.- La interrupción de la prescripción a favor de alguno de los acreedores solidarios aprovecha a todos, y las causas que interrumpen la prescripción respecto de uno de los deudores solidarios, la interrumpen también respecto de los otros.

Sin embargo, si el acreedor, consintiendo en la división de la deuda respecto de uno de los deudores solidarios sólo exigiere de él la parte que le corresponda, no se tendrá por interrumpida la prescripción respecto de los demás.

Artículo 1748.- La interrupción de la prescripción contra el deudor principal produce los mismos efectos contra su fiador.

A new term of ***Debt Cancellation*** starts, in the case of acknowledgement of the obligations, from the day in which ***the acknowledgement*** occurs; if the document is renewed, from the date of the new title, and if the term of the discharge of the obligation is extended, from the due date of the new term or extension.

Article 1747.- The suspension of the ***Debt Cancellation*** in favour of any one of the general creditors is available to all **creditors**, and the causes that suspend the ***Debt Cancellation*** for one of the joint debtors, also suspend it for the other ***debtors***.

However, if the creditor, consenting to the separation of the debt for one joint and several debtor, ***and*** only demands of ***this debtor*** the part that corresponds to ***this debtor***, this is not considered a suspension of ***Debt Cancellation*** in relation to the other ***debtors***.

Article 1748.- The suspension of the ***Debt Cancellation*** against the principal debtor produces the same effects against their guarantors.

PART 12 – Income Tax & IVA

Federal Income Tax Law
Title 3
Articles 79 & 86,

Income Tax Regulations
Title II
Article 25, and
Title IV
Article 121,
&

IVA Regulations
Chapter 1
Article 20 and
Chapter III
Article 33

Relevance to a Condominium

Significant changes to the Income Tax laws made in 2014, coupled with tightening enforcement by *SAT – Servicio de Administración Tributaria* (Tax Administration Service), have made it necessary for condominiums to register with the tax authority, open a bank account, file tax reports, and comply with tax laws.

SAT is an official agency of the *Secretaría de Hacienda y Crédito Público* (Department of Finance and Public Credit, generally referred to as "*Hacienda*"). It's charged with applying and enforcing federal tax and customs legislation.

The good news is that condominiums are considered a nonprofit by the tax department, and are exempt from charging IVA (the 16% value-added tax) on condo fees charged to the owners. This status is achieved by properly registering with Hacienda, filing regularly with the tax department, and complying with the tax regulations.

A condo does not have to remit taxes during the year, unless they have direct employees. It must file a tax return at the end of the calendar year, but will not be charged income tax except in certain situations (which usually can be avoided).

It must also render monthly reports on expenses paid to individuals or companies for goods or services.

For practical steps on registering a condo with *Hacienda*, and information on how the taxes are applied, see our companion book, the "***Jalisco Condo Manual – Second Edition***."

Versions of Laws Used

Codes and laws are living documents that are amended frequently by the level of government that issued them.

This section contains excerpts from:

> the *Ley del Impuesto Sobre la Renta* (Income Tax Law), that took effect on **January 1, 2014**, and was last amended on **January 1, 2014**;

> the *Reglamento de la Ley del Impuesto Sobre la Renta* (Regulations for the Income Tax Law), that took effect on **December 4, 2006**, and was last amended on **December 4, 2006**; and

the *Reglamento de la Ley del Impuesto Al Valor Agregado* (Regulations for the Law of Value-Added Tax), that took effect on **October 17, 2003**, last amended on ***September 25, 2014***.

Sections of the Laws Used

The excerpt from the **Income Tax Law** translated in this section is from: *Título III*:

Título III (Title III) is titled "*Del Régimen de las Personas Morales con Fines No Lucrativos*" (The System of Legal Entities and Nonprofits).

The excerpts from the **Regulations for the Income Tax Law** translated in this section are from: *Título II* and *Título IV*:

Título II (Title II) is titled "*De Las Personas Morales*" (Legal Entities).

Título IV (Title IV) is titled "*De Las Personas Física*" (Individuals).

The excerpts from the **Regulations for the Law of Value-Added Tax** translated in this section are from: *Capítulo I* and *Capítulo III*:

Capítulo I (Chapter I) is titled "*Disposiciones Generales*" (General Provisions), and

Capítulo III (Chapter III) is titled "*De la Prestación de Servicios*" (Provision of Services).

LEY DEL IMPUESTO SOBRE LA RENTA

TÍTULO III – DEL RÉGIMEN DE LAS PERSONAS MORALES CON FINES NO LUCRATIVOS

ESTE TÍTULO NO TIENE CAPÍTULOS

Artículo 79. No son contribuyentes del impuesto sobre la renta, las siguientes personas morales:

[Los subpárrafos I a través de XVII se han omitido]

XVIII. Asociaciones civiles de colonos y las asociaciones civiles que se dediquen exclusivamente a la administración de un inmueble de propiedad en condominio.

[Los subpárrafos XIX a través de XXVI se han omitido]

Las personas morales a que se refieren las fracciones V, VI, VII, IX, X, XI, XIII, XVI, XVII, XVIII, XIX, XX, XXIV y XXV de este artículo, así como las personas morales y fideicomisos autorizados para recibir donativos deducibles de impuestos, y las sociedades de inversión a que se refiere este Título,

INCOME TAX LAW

TITLE III – THE SYSTEM OF LEGAL ENTITIES AND NONPROFITS

NO CHAPTERS – Legal Entities & Nonprofits

Article 79.- The following legal entities **[as opposed to individuals]** are exempt from income tax **[considered a nonprofit]**:

[sub-paragraphs I through XVII have been omitted]

XVIII. Neighbourhood associations and civil associations that are **dedicated exclusively to the administration of a condominium property** **[current interpretation of this by SAT expands** *"civil associations...administration of a condominium property"* **to also include a legally constituted condominium regime – see the next translation of Article 25 from the Regulations]**.

[sub-paragraphs XIX through XXVI have been omitted]

The legal entities referred to in subparagraphs V, VI, VII, IX, X, XI, XIII, XVI, XVII, **XVIII [a condominium – see above]**, XIX, XX, XXIV and XXV of this article, as well as the legal entities and trusts authorized to receive tax-deductible donations, and the investment companies referred to in this Title,

considerarán remanente distribuible, aun cuando no lo hayan entregado en efectivo o en bienes a sus integrantes o socios, el importe de las omisiones de 1.-ingresos o 2.-las compras no realizadas e 3.- indebidamente registradas; 4.-las erogaciones que efectúen y no sean deducibles en los términos del Título IV de esta Ley, salvo cuando dicha circunstancia se deba a que éstas no reúnen los requisitos de la fracción IV del artículo 147 (requisitos deducciones) de la misma; los préstamos que hagan a sus socios o integrantes, o a los cónyuges, ascendientes o descendientes en línea recta de dichos socios o integrantes salvo en el caso de préstamos a los socios o integrantes de las sociedades cooperativas de ahorro y préstamo a que se refiere la fracción XIII de este artículo. Tratándose de préstamos que en los términos de este párrafo se consideren remanente distribuible, su importe se disminuirá de los remanentes distribuibles que la persona moral distribuya a sus socios o integrantes.

must consider as a distributable balance **[a *distributable balance* is a taxable remainder disbursed to members or shareholders of a company – a nonprofit can have an *implied* distributable balance in certain circumstances, and this becomes taxable at the highest tax rate (see the *"Jalisco Condo Manual – Second Edition"* for more details)]**, even though they have not delivered *this distributable balance* in cash or goods to their members or associates, the total sum of the *unreported* 1.-income or 2.-unrealised purchases and 3.-improperly recorded *purchases*; 4.-expenses that are not deductible under the terms of Title IV of this Law **[income taxes payable by individuals – main body of the income tax law]**, except when these circumstances do not meet the requirements of subparagraph IV of Article 147 (requirements for deductions) of *Title IV*; the loans made to *the entity's* associates or members, or to the spouses, forebears or direct descendents of the aforementioned associates or members, except in the case of loans made to the associates or members of savings and loan societies to which subparagraph XIII of this article refers **[institutions and civil societies for managing funds, and savings and loan societies]**. For loans that are considered to be a distributable balance under the terms of this paragraph, *the entity's* total distributable balance must be decreased by that *amount* which the legal entity disburses to its associates or members.

En el caso en el que se determine remanente distribuible en los términos del párrafo anterior, la persona moral de que se trate enterará como impuesto a su cargo el impuesto que resulte de aplicar sobre dicho remanente distribuible, la tasa máxima para aplicarse sobre el excedente del límite inferior que establece la tarifa contenida en el artículo 152 (35%) de esta Ley, en cuyo caso se considerará como impuesto definitivo, debiendo efectuar el entero correspondiente a más tardar en el mes de febrero del año siguiente a aquél en el que ocurra cualquiera de los supuestos a que se refiere dicho párrafo.

[Artículos 80 a través de 85 se han omitido porque no se aplican a los condominios]

Artículo 86. Las personas morales a que se refiere este Título, además de las obligaciones establecidas en otros artículos de esta Ley, tendrán las siguientes:

I. Llevar los sistemas contables de conformidad con el Código Fiscal de la Federación, su Reglamento y el Reglamento de esta Ley y efectuar registros en los mismos respecto de sus operaciones.

II. Expedir y recabar los comprobantes fiscales que acrediten las enajenaciones y erogaciones que efectúen, los servicios que presten o el otorgamiento del uso o goce temporal de bienes.

If a distributable balance under the terms of the previous paragraph is determined *to exist*, the legal entity must report as tax payable *the amount* which results from applying to this distributable balance the maximum tax rate applicable (35%) as established by the tariff contained in Article 152 of this Law **[the table of income tax rates based on ranges of income – this is the highest rate]**, *having to pay the entire amount* no later than the month of February of the year following the *year* in which any of the conditions referred to in *the previous* paragraph occurred, in which case, it is considered to be a final tax.

[Articles 80 through 85 have been omitted because they do not apply to condominiums]

Article 86.- The legal entities referred to in this Title **[nonprofits, such as a condo]**, in addition to the obligations established in other articles of this Law, have the following *obligations*:

I. *To use* accounting systems in accordance with the *Código Fiscal de la Federación* (Federal Fiscal Code), its regulations, and the regulations of this Law, and to *keep* records of its operation in this same way **[in accordance with the Federal Fiscal Code]**.

II. To issue and obtain the supporting financial documents that correspond to the sales and expenses that *the legal entity* has, the services that they render, or the use or temporary enjoyment of goods that they grant *to others* **[for example, rentals]**.

III. Presentar en las oficinas autorizadas a más tardar el día 15 de febrero de cada año, declaración en la que se determine el remanente distribuible y la proporción que de este concepto corresponda a cada integrante.

IV. Proporcionar a sus integrantes constancia y comprobante fiscal en el que se señale el monto del remanente distribuible, en su caso.

V. Expedir las constancias y el comprobante fiscal y proporcionar la información a que se refiere la fracción III del artículo 76 de esta Ley; retener y enterar el impuesto a cargo de terceros y exigir el comprobante respectivo, cuando hagan pagos a terceros y estén obligados a ello en los términos de esta Ley. Deberán cumplir con las obligaciones a que se refiere el artículo 94 de la misma Ley, cuando hagan pagos que a la vez sean ingresos en los términos del Capítulo I del Título IV del presente ordenamiento.

III. To present in the authorised offices, no later than the 15th day of February each year, a declaration in which the distributable balance and the portion that corresponds to each member are stated.

IV. Provide its members with a written declaration *with* the supporting financial documents in which the amount of the distributable balance is indicated, if any.

V. Issue a written declaration *along with* the supporting financial documents, and provide the information referred to in subparagraph III of Article 76 of this Law **[requirement to issue tax receipts for sources of income]**; retain and report the tax payable by third parties, and demand the respective supporting documents, when *the legal entity* makes payments to third parties, and they are obliged to do this under the terms of this Law. *The legal entity* must fulfill the obligations referred to in Article 94 of this Law **[see below]** when they make payments that are at the same time income **[for third parties]** under the terms of Chapter I of Title IV of this Law **[section on income from salaries and the provision of personal services – contains Article 94 mentioned above]**.

Los sindicatos obreros y los organismos que los agrupen quedan relevados de cumplir con las obligaciones establecidas en las fracciones I y II de este artículo, excepto por aquellas actividades que de realizarse por otra persona quedarían comprendidas en el artículo 16 del Código Fiscal de la Federación. Quedan relevadas de cumplir con las obligaciones a que se refieren las fracciones III y IV de este artículo las personas señaladas en el artículo 79 de esta Ley que no determinen remanente distribuible.

[Los últimos seis párrafos de este artículo se han omitido porque no se aplican a los condominios]

Labour unions, and entities formed by groups, are relieved from fulfilling the obligations established in subparagraphs I and II of this article, except for activities that are carried out by someone else and would be included in Article 16 of the *Código Fiscal de la Federación* (Federal Fiscal Code) **[definitions of business activities]**. *Nonprofits* **[such as condos]** indicated in Article 79 of this Law **[this article]** that *have calculated no* distributable balance, are relieved from fulfilling the obligations referred to in subparagraphs III and IV of this article.

[The last six paragraphs of this article have been omitted because they do not apply to condominiums]

<u>**REGLAMENTO DE LA LEY DEL IMPUESTO SOBRE LA RENTA**</u>	<u>**REGULATIONS FOR THE INCOME TAX LAW**</u>

<u>**TÍTULO II – DE LAS PERSONAS MORALES**</u>

<u>**TITLE II – LEGAL ENTITIES**</u>

CAPÍTULO II – De las Deducciones

CHAPTER II – Deductions

SECCIÓN I – De las Deducciones en General

SECTION I – Deductions in General

Artículo 25. Los contribuyentes que paguen el impuesto a su cargo en los términos del Título II de la Ley, que para la realización de las actividades por las que paguen dicho impuesto utilicen inmuebles sujetos al régimen de propiedad en condominio, podrán deducir la parte proporcional que les corresponda de los gastos comunes que se hubieren realizado en relación con el inmueble, siempre que además de los requisitos que establece la Ley, se cumpla con lo siguiente:

Article 25. Contributors that pay the tax *owed by them* under the terms of Title II of *this* Law **[this title – Legal Entities – a condominium regime is a legal entity]**, that <u>**use property subject to a condominium regime**</u> to carry out the activities for which they pay this tax, can deduct the proportional percentage corresponding to the common expenses made in relation to the *condo* property, provided that, in addition to the requirements that are established by Law, they comply with the following:

I. Que los gastos de conservación y mantenimiento sean realizados en nombre y representación de la asamblea general de condóminos por un administrador que cuente con facultades para actuar con el carácter mencionado, otorgado por dicha asamblea.

I. That the expenses for repairs and maintenance are made in the name of, and on behalf of, the general assembly of condominium owners by an administrator that has the authority to act *in this capacity*, granted by this assembly **[make sure you have a copy of the registered minutes of the most recent annual ordinary assembly – this proves the appointment of the Administrator for this year]**.

II. Que el pago de las cuotas de conservación y mantenimiento las realicen los condóminos mediante depósito en la cuenta bancaria que haya constituido la asamblea general de condóminos para tal efecto.

II. That the payment of fees for repairs and maintenance has been made by the condominium owners by means of being deposited in a bank account that has been established by the general assembly of condominium owners for this purpose.

III. Que los comprobantes que amparen los gastos comunes de conservación y mantenimiento estén a nombre de la asamblea general de condóminos o del administrador.

IV. Que el administrador recabe los comprobantes relativos a los gastos comunes, que reúnan los requisitos que establece el artículo 29-A del Código Fiscal de la Federación y entregue a cada condómino una constancia por periodos mensuales en la que se especifique:

a) Los números correspondientes a los comprobantes mencionados y el concepto que ampara cada comprobante, el monto total de dichos comprobantes y el impuesto al valor agregado respectivo.

b) La parte proporcional que corresponde al condómino de que se trate, del gasto total, conforme al por ciento de indiviso que represente cada unidad de propiedad exclusiva en el condominio de que se trate. No se considerará en el total del gasto, el impuesto al valor agregado que se hubiere causado sobre dicho gasto, excepto cuando el contribuyente por la actividad que realice en el inmueble, se encuentre exento del pago del impuesto al valor agregado.

Igualmente, el administrador deberá entregar a cada condómino una copia de los comprobantes.

III. That the supporting documents that back up the common expenses for repairs and maintenance are in the name of the general assembly of condominium owners, or of the Administrator.

IV. That the Administrator obtains the supporting documents corresponding to the common expenses, that they meet the requirements established by Article 29-A of the *Código Fiscal de la Federación* (Federal Fiscal Code) **[requirement for electronic tax receipts or *facturas*]**, and ***the Administrator*** delivers to each condominium owner a monthly written declaration ***in the manner*** specified ***below***:

a) The numbers corresponding to the supporting documents mentioned ***above*** and a ***description of the expense*** that backs up each supporting document, the total amount of these supporting documents, and the corresponding value-added tax ***paid*** **[IVA]**.

b) The proportional percentage of the total ***reported*** expenses that corresponds to ***each*** condominium owner, in accordance with the percentage of undivided property **[condo rights]** that each ***private unit*** represents in the condominium. The value-added tax **[IVA]** ***applicable to*** these expenses must not be considered in the total of the expenses, except when the ***supplier*** of the activity ***that was*** carried out on the ***condo*** property **[goods or services provided to the condo]**, ***is*** exempt from payment of value-added tax.

As well, the Administrator must deliver a copy of the supporting documents to each condominium owner.

V. En el caso de que el administrador reciba contraprestaciones por sus servicios de administración, deberá expedir un comprobante que reúna los requisitos previstos en el artículo 29-A del Código Fiscal de la Federación, a nombre de la asamblea general de condóminos, el cual servirá de base para elaborar las constancias en los términos establecidos en la fracción IV de este artículo.

VI. La documentación y registros contables deberán conservarse por la asamblea de condóminos o, en su defecto, por los condóminos que opten por deducir los gastos comunes en los términos del presente artículo.

No se podrá optar por efectuar la deducción de los gastos comunes en los términos del presente artículo, cuando las personas que presten los servicios de administración carezcan de facultades para actuar en nombre y representación de la asamblea general de condóminos.

V. In the event that the administrator receives remuneration for their management services, they must issue a supporting document that ***meets*** the requirements of Article 29-A of the *Código Fiscal de la Federación* (Federal Fiscal Code) **[requirement for electronic tax receipts or *facturas*]** in the name of the general assembly of condominium owners, which must serve as the basis to draw up the written declarations under the terms established in subparagraph IV of this article **[the previous one]**.

VI. The documentation and accounting records must be kept in good order **[accurate and up to date]** for the assembly of condominium owners or, in the ***absence of such documentation and records***, by the condominium owners that choose to deduct the common expenses under the terms of this article.

It is not ***possible*** to deduct common expenses as tax credits under the terms of this article when the persons that perform the management services lack the authority to act in the name of, and on behalf of, the general assembly of condominium owners **[it is important to have copies of the registered minutes of each Annual Ordinary Assembly showing the appointment of the Administrator for a one-year term, as well as the granting of powers to them for legal and administrative representation]**.

TÍTULO IV – DE LAS PERSONAS FÍSICA

Disposiciones Generales

Artículo 121. Los contribuyentes que paguen el impuesto a su cargo en los términos del Título IV, Capítulos II y III de la Ley, que para la realización de las actividades por las que paguen dicho impuesto utilicen inmuebles sujetos al régimen de propiedad en condominio, podrán deducir los gastos comunes que se hubieren realizado en relación con el inmueble, siempre que se cumpla con los requisitos a que se refiere el artículo 25 de este Reglamento.

TITLE IV – INDIVIDUALS

General Provisions [Individuals]

Article 121. Contributors who pay the tax *owed by them* under the terms of Title IV **[this title – Individuals – as opposed to a legal entity such as a condo, a company, or an association]**, Chapters II and III of *this* law **[Income From Business & Professional Activities, and Income From Renting & Granting the Temporary Use or Enjoyment of Real Estate In General]**, who <u>use property subject to a condominium regime</u> to carry out the activities for which they pay this tax, can deduct the common expenses made in relation to the *condo* property, provided that they comply with the requirements referred to in Article 25 of these Regulations **[the previous translation]**.

REGLAMENTO DE LA LEY DEL IMPUESTO AL VALOR AGREGADO

CAPÍTULO I – Disposiciones Generales

Artículo 20. Para los efectos de las disposiciones que establece la Ley en materia de acreditamiento, éste podrá ser realizado por los contribuyentes que realicen actividades por las que se deba pagar el impuesto en inmuebles sujetos al régimen de propiedad en condominio, en la parte proporcional que les corresponda del impuesto trasladado en las operaciones que amparen los gastos comunes relativos al inmueble de que se trate, siempre que además de los requisitos que establece la Ley, se cumpla con lo siguiente:

I. Que los gastos de conservación y mantenimiento sean realizados en nombre y representación de la asamblea general de condóminos por un administrador que cuente con facultades para actuar con el carácter mencionado otorgado por dicha asamblea;

II. Que el pago de las cuotas de conservación y mantenimiento las realicen los condóminos mediante depósito en la cuenta bancaria que haya constituido la asamblea general de condóminos para tal efecto;

REGULATIONS FOR THE LAW OF VALUE-ADDED TAX [VA]

CHAPTER I – General Provisions [IVA]

Article 20. The effects of the provisions established *in the* Law *of Value-Added Tax* regarding tax credits *apply to* taxpayers that carry out activities for which they must pay tax on **property subject to a condominium regime**, in the proportional percentage that corresponds to *each of* them, of the transferred tax **[IVA is payable by the final consumer of goods or services, and tax credits are transferred along the line to this final tax payer]** from the operations that support the common expenses for the property *in question*, provided that, in addition to the requirements established by the Law *of Value-Added Tax*, they comply with the following:

I. That the expenses for repairs and maintenance, are made in the name of, and on behalf of, the general assembly of condominium owners by an administrator that has the authority to act *in this capacity*, granted by this assembly **[make sure you have a copy of the registered minutes of the most recent annual ordinary assembly – this proves the appointment of the Administrator for this year]**;

II. That the payment of fees for repairs and maintenance has been made by the condominium owners by means of being deposited in a bank account that has been established by the general assembly of condominium owners for this purpose;

III. Que los comprobantes fiscales que amparen los gastos comunes de conservación y mantenimiento se expidan a nombre de la asamblea general de condóminos o del administrador;

Fracción reformada DOF 25-09-2014

IV. Que el administrador recabe los comprobantes fiscales relativos a los gastos comunes y entregue a cada condómino una constancia por periodos mensuales en la que se especifique:

Párrafo reformado DOF 25-09-2014

a) Los números correspondientes a los comprobantes mencionados y el concepto que ampara cada comprobante, el monto total de dichos comprobantes y el impuesto respectivo, y

b) La parte proporcional que corresponde al condómino, tanto del gasto total como del impuesto correspondiente, conforme al por ciento de indiviso que represente cada unidad de propiedad exclusiva en el condominio de que se trate.

Igualmente, el administrador deberá entregar a cada condómino una copia de los comprobantes.

III. That the supporting financial documents that back up the common expenses for repairs and maintenance are in the name of the general assembly of condominium owners, or of the Administrator;

Sub-paragrah modified 25-09-2014

IV. That the Administrator obtains the supporting financial documents corresponding to the common expenses, and ***the Administrator*** delivers to each condominium owner a monthly written declaration ***in the manner*** specified ***below***:

Paragraph modified 25-09-2014

a) The numbers corresponding to the supporting documents mentioned ***above*** and a ***description of the expense*** that backs up each supporting document, the total amount of these supporting documents, and the corresponding value-added tax ***paid* [IVA]**, and

b) The proportional percentage of the total ***reported*** expenses that correspond to ***each*** condominium owner, in accordance with the percentage of undivided property **[condo rights]** that each ***private unit*** represents in the condominium.

As well, the Administrator must deliver a copy of the supporting documents to each condominium owner.

V. En el caso de que el administrador reciba contraprestaciones por sus servicios de administración deberá expedir un comprobante fiscal a nombre de la asamblea general de condóminos, el cual servirá de base para elaborar las constancias en los términos establecidos en la fracción IV de este artículo, y

Fracción reformada DOF 25-09-2014

VI. La documentación y registros contables deberán conservarse por la asamblea de condóminos o, en su defecto, por los condóminos que opten por el acreditamiento de los gastos comunes en los términos del presente artículo.

No se podrá optar por efectuar el acreditamiento del impuesto que corresponda a los gastos comunes en los términos del presente artículo, cuando las personas que presten los servicios de administración carezcan de facultades para actuar en nombre y representación de la asamblea general de condóminos.

V. In the event that the administrator receives remuneration for their management services, they must issue a supporting fiscal document in the name of the general assembly of condominium owners, which must serve as the basis to draw up the written declarations under the terms established in subparagraph IV of this article **[the previous one]**, and

Sub-paragraph modified 25-09-2014

VI. The documentation and accounting records must be kept in good order **[accurate and up to date]** for the assembly of condominium owners or, in its *absence of such documentation and records*, by the condominium owners that choose to deduct the common expenses under the terms of this article.

It is not *possible* to deduct common expenses as tax credits under the terms of this article, when the persons that perform the management services lack the authority to act in the name of and on behalf of the general assembly of condominium owners **[it is important to have copies of the registered minutes of each Annual Ordinary Assembly showing the appointment of the Administrator for a one-year term, as well as the granting of powers to them for legal and administrative representation].**

CAPÍTULO III – De la Prestación de Servicios

Artículo 33. Para los efectos del artículo 14 de la Ley, tratándose de las cuotas que aporten los propietarios de inmuebles sujetos al régimen de propiedad en condominio o a cualquier otra modalidad en la que se realicen gastos comunes, que se destinen para la constitución o el incremento de los fondos con los cuales se solventan dichos gastos, el impuesto se causa sólo por la parte que se destine a cubrir las contraprestaciones de la persona que tenga a su cargo la administración del inmueble.

CHAPTER III – Provision of Services

Article 33. For the assessed fees that are contributed by the owners of **property subject to a condominium regime**, or by any other method in which common expenses come about, ***when these fees*** are used for the creation of, or to increase, the funds which ***pay*** these ***common*** expenses, ***value-added tax*** [IVA] brought about by Article 14 of the Law ***of Value-Added Tax*** [**provision of independent services**], is only ***payable*** on the portion that is used to cover the remuneration of the person that has the responsibility for the administration of the property.

PART 13 – Rules for Public Property Auctions

Jalisco Code of Civil Procedures
Title 8
Articles 550 – 583

Relevance to a Condominium

When an owner has become significantly delinquent in their fees, or has caused significant problems in the condo, the condo administration can go before a judge, and apply to have the private unit sold at public auction under the terms of **Civil Code Article 1032** (see *Part 3 – The Jalisco Condo Law*).

In the case of a delinquent owner, the condo can recover the overdue fees. In all cases, the condo can recover the costs of the legal proceeding.

Once the auction has been approved by a local judge, it follows the rules laid out in the *Código de Procedimientos Civiles del Estado de Jalisco* (Code of Civil Procedures for the State of Jalisco). This code supplements the Civil Code.

For practical steps on initiating such a lawsuit, and the steps and time frames involved in the legal process, see our companion book, the *"Jalisco Condo Manual – Second Edition."*

Versions of Laws Used

Codes and laws are living documents that are amended frequently by the level of government that issued them.

This section contains excerpts from the *Código de Procedimientos Civiles del Estado de Jalisco* (Code of Civil Procedures for the State of Jalisco), that took effect on **January 1, 1939**, and was last amended on **November 29, 2014**.

Sections of the Laws Used

The excerpt from the **Jalisco Code of Civil Procedures** translated in this section is from: *Título Octavo*:

> *Título Octavo* (Title Eight) is titled *"De la Ejecución de las Sentencias"* (Execution of Judgements).

| CÓDIGO DE PROCEDIMIENTOS CIVILES DEL ESTADO DE JALISCO | CODE OF CIVIL PROCEDURES OF THE STATE OF JALISCO |

CÓDIGO DE PROCEDIMIENTOS CIVILES DEL ESTADO DE JALISCO

TÍTULO OCTAVO – DE LA EJECUCIÓN DE LAS SENTENCIAS

CAPÍTULO IV – De los Remates

Artículo 550. Toda venta que conforme a la ley deba hacerse en subasta o almoneda, se ajustará a las disposiciones contenidas en este Título, salvo los casos en que la ley disponga otra cosa.

Artículo 551.- Todo remate de bienes raíces será público y deberá celebrarse en el Juzgado en que actúe el Juez que fuere competente para la ejecución.

Artículo 552.- No podrá procederse al remate de bienes raíces, sin que previamente se haya pedido al Registro Público de la Propiedad, certificado de libertad o de los gravámenes del predio y sin que se haya citado a los acreedores que aparezcan de dicho certificado; éste comprenderá los últimos diez años, pero si en autos obrare ya otro certificado, sólo se pedirá al Registro el relativo al período transcurrido desde la fecha de aquél, hasta la en que se decretó la venta. En defecto de los datos que pueda ministrar el Registro Público de la Propiedad, deberá el Juez recabar previamente constancia de la Oficina Catastral respectiva para cerciorarse, al menos por este medio, de que la persona contra quien se pretende fincar el remate, es la misma en cuyo favor estuviere empadronada la finca de que se trata; si esto no fuere así, el remate no se llevará a efecto.

CODE OF CIVIL PROCEDURES OF THE STATE OF JALISCO

TITLE EIGHT – EXECUTION OF JUDGEMENTS

CHAPTER IV – Auction Sales

Article 550.- Every sale, which must be done by public auction or liquidation according to law, must follow the provisions contained in this Title, except in cases in which the law stipulates something else.

Article 551. Every auction sale of real estate must be public, and must be carried out in the courthouse in which the Judge that has authority for the enforcement *of the judgement carries out their judicial acts*.

Article 552. An auction sale of real estate cannot proceed without ordering a certificate of freedom from liens and property taxes from the Public Registry of Property, and without making an appointment with the creditors that appear on this certificate; this *certificate* is understood to *cover* the last ten years, but if another certificate has already been used in *a court order*, it is only necessary to order *a certificate* from the *Public* Registry *covering* the period from the date of the previous one until the date the auction has been decreed. In the absence of a *certificate* from the Public Registry of Property, the Judge must obtain previous records from the corresponding Land Registry Office to make certain, at least by this means, that the person against whom the property in the auction sale is claimed, is the same one in whose *name* the property in question is registered; if this is not *the case*, the auction sale cannot take place.

Artículo 553.- Si del certificado aparecieren gravámenes, se hará saber a los acreedores el estado de la ejecución para que intervengan en la subasta de los bienes, si les conviniere.

La citación de los acreedores se hará personalmente en su domicilio, que deberá indicar el ejecutante si le fuere conocido; en caso contrario, se llevará a efecto en las mismas convocatorias del remate.

Artículo 554.- Los acreedores citados, conforme al artículo anterior, tendrán derecho:

I. Para intervenir en el acto del remate, pudiendo hacer al Juez las observaciones que estimen oportunas para garantizar sus derechos;

II. Para recurrir el auto de aprobación del remate, en su caso; y

III. Cuando el estado de los autos lo permita, para nombrar a su costa un perito que con los nombrados por el ejecutante y el ejecutado, practique el avalúo de la cosa. Nunca disfrutarán de este derecho después de practicado el avalúo por los peritos de las partes o el tercero en discordia, ni cuando la valorización se haga por otros medios.

Artículo 555.- El avalúo se practicará observando las reglas establecidas para la prueba pericial por este Código.

Article 553. If liens show up on the certificate, the status of the legal process must be made known to the creditors **named on the certificate** so that they can take part in the auction of the goods, if convenient for them.

The summons of the creditors must be made in person at their domicile, **and** must indicate the petitioner of the lawsuit, if known; otherwise, **notification** becomes effective with the announcement of the auction sale.

Article 554. The creditors summoned in accordance with the previous article have the right:

I. To take part in the process of the auction sale, being able to make observations to the Judge that they regard as **appropriate** to protect their rights;

II. To appeal the court order approving the auction sale, **for their reasons**; and

III. When the condition of the court orders permits, to name an expert at **the creditor's** expense who, with those named by the petitioner of the lawsuit and the debtor, **carry out** the appraisal of the **property being auctioned**. They cannot exercise this right after the appraisal **has been carried out** by the experts of the **involved** parties or third parties in disagreement, nor when the appraisal is made by other means.

Article 555. Appraisals must be made following the rules established by this Code for expert testimony.

Artículo 556.- Justipreciados los bienes, si fueren raíces se anunciará su venta señalando día y hora para la almoneda, por medio de edictos que se publicarán por dos veces de diez en diez días, en el Boletín Judicial o en el Periódico Oficial, y en un Diario de los de mayor circulación, a juicio del juez. A petición de las partes, y a su costa, el juez puede usar, además de los mencionados, algún otro medio de publicidad para convocar postores. También previo a petición del ejecutante, se podrá comunicar en el anuncio de la venta que se admitirán postores que ofrezcan el pago del remanente del precio en los plazos y condiciones que éste señale.

Article 556. Once the property has been appraised, if it was real estate, the sale must be advertised indicating the day and hour of the auction, through proclamations published twice, ten days apart, in the Law Journal or in the Official Newspaper, and in a daily newspaper of large circulation, ***as determined by*** the judge. At the request of the parties, and at their expense, the judge can use, in addition to those mentioned, other means of publicity to invite bidders. Also ***allowed***, at the request of the petitioner of the lawsuit, it is possible to say in the auction announcement that bidders will be admitted ***to the auction*** who offer payment of the remainder of the price, under terms and conditions indicated ***in the announcement***.

Artículo 557.- Antes de aprobarse en definitiva el remate o declararse la adjudicación el deudor podrá librar sus bienes pagando principal y costas. Después de fincado quedará irrevocable la venta, salvo pacto o convenio en contrario de las partes y el adjudicatario, el cual en todo caso deberá constar por escrito y ratificado ante la autoridad judicial.

Article 557. Before the auction sale is finally approved or declared as being awarded **[to a successful bidder]**, the debtor can free their goods by paying the principal ***amount owed plus*** the legal costs. After ***it has been finalised***, the sale becomes irrevocable, except by a pact or agreement to the contrary ***between*** the parties and the successful bidder, which in any case must be recorded in writing and ratified before the judicial authority.

Artículo 558.- Si los bienes raíces estuvieren situados en diversos lugares, en todos éstos se publicarán los edictos en los sitios de costumbre y en las puertas de los juzgados respectivos.

En el caso a que se refiere este artículo, se ampliará el término de publicación de los edictos, concediéndose el que el Juez estime necesario en atención a la distancia y a la dificultad de las comunicaciones.

Article 558. If real estate property is located in several places, the proclamations must be published in all of these **[places]** in customary locations, and on the doors of the respective courthouses.

In the situation to which this article refers, the Judge is allowed to increase the term of publication of the proclamations, if he considers it necessary in view of the distance and difficulty of communication.

Artículo 559.- Será postura legal, la que cubra las dos terceras partes del avalúo o del precio fijado a la finca hipotecada por los contratantes, la cual se exhibirá siempre mediante billete de depósito.

Artículo 560.- Para tomar parte en la subasta, los licitadores deberán presentar por escrito su postura y consignar previamente, en la Secretaría de Finanzas del Estado o Delegación correspondiente, a disposición del juzgado, una cantidad igual por lo menos al veinticinco por ciento del importe total de la postura legal para el remate, sin cuyos requisitos no serán admitidos. Se devolverán los certificados de depósito a sus respectivos dueños acto continuo al remate, excepto la del mejor postor que se conservará en depósito como garantía del cumplimiento de sus obligaciones y, en su caso, como parte del precio de la venta.

Artículo 561.- El ejecutante podrá tomar parte en la subasta y mejorar las posturas que se hicieren, sin necesidad de consignar el depósito prevenido en el artículo anterior, si el importe de su crédito, reconocido en la sentencia cubre el veinticinco por ciento a que el citado artículo se refiere.

Artículo 562.- La postura deberá contener:

I. Las generales del postor;

II. El precio que se ofrezca por la finca y la forma de cubrirlo;

III. El interés que deba causar la suma que se queda reconociendo, en el caso de que el ejecutante así lo aceptare;

Article 559. The *auction value* must be two-thirds **[2/3]** of the appraised value, or the fixed price of the property mortgaged by the contracting parties, which must be covered by means of a *bid bond*.

Article 560. To take part in the auction, bidders must *assign their bid bond* beforehand, and present their bid in writing to the Department of State Finance or corresponding local office **[of the Department]**, to the order of the court, in an amount equal to at least twenty-five percent **[25%]** of the total amount of the *auction value* for the auction sale. If they do not meet these requirements, they are not *allowed to take part*. The *bid bonds* must be returned to their respective owners immediately after the auction sale, except the one belonging to the highest bidder, which must be kept on deposit as a guarantee of the fulfilments of *the bidder's* obligations and, *possibly*, as part of the price of the sale.

Article 561. The petitioner of the lawsuit can take part in the auction, and increase the bids that are made, without the necessity of assigning a *bid bond* as mentioned in the previous article, if the total amount of *the petitioner's* claim, identified in the judgement, is covered by the twenty-five percent **[25%]** *of the auction value* referred to in the previous article **[it is less than this]**.

Article 562. A bid must contain:

I. The personal data of the bidder;

II. The price that is offered for the property, and the means of providing the funds;

III. The interest that *applies to* the remaining amount, in the event that the petitioner of the lawsuit agrees.

IV. La sumisión al Juez que practica el remate para que haga cumplir el contrato; y

V. La constancia de haberse hecho el depósito a que se refiere el artículo 560.

Artículo 563.- El postor no puede rematar para un tercero sino con poder y cláusula especial, quedando prohibido hacer posturas reservándose la facultad de declarar después el nombre de la persona para quien se hizo.

Artículo 564.- Desde que se anuncia el remate y durante éste, se pondrán de manifiesto las constancias de autos, escrituras, planos, avalúos y demás documentos que hubiere; y estarán a la vista los avalúos.

Artículo 565.- El juez ejecutor decidirá de plano toda cuestión que se suscite durante la subasta y de sus resoluciones no se admitirá recurso alguno, a menos que la ley disponga otra cosa.

Artículo 566.- El día del remate, a la hora señalada, el juez ordenará al secretario levante certificación de la publicación de los edictos, pasará lista de los postores presentados; hecho lo anterior, procederá al remate sin admitir nuevos postores. Enseguida revisarán las propuestas presentadas desechando, desde luego, las que no tengan postura legal y los demás requisitos que mencione el artículo 562.

IV. The submission to the Judge that uses the auction sale to enforce the settlement; and

V. The written declaration of having made the ***bid bond*** referred to in Article 560.

Article 563. The bidder cannot act for a third party without a power of attorney ***that includes a special stipulation***, and is prohibited from making bids that conceal the ability to declare afterwards the name of the person for whom the bid was made.

Article 564. From the time the auction sale is announced, and during ***the auction***, the written declarations of court proceedings, public documents, plans, appraisals, and other documents which exist must be ***made public***, and the appraisals must be on view.

Article 565. The presiding judge makes the final decision on all issues that arise during the auction, and no appeal of these decisions is allowed, unless the law provides differently.

Article 566. ***On*** the day of the auction sale, at the appointed hour, the judge must order the Secretary to ***certify*** the publication of the proclamations, and conduct a roll call of the bidders present; ***having done this***, the auction sale must proceed without admitting new bidders. ***The Judge*** must check the proposals presented right away, discarding immediately those that do not have a ***bid bond*** and the other requirements mentioned in Article 562.

Artículo 567.- Calificadas de buenas las posturas, el juez las leerá en voz alta por sí mismo o mandará que las lea el secretario, para que los postores presentes puedan mejorarlas. Si hubiere varias posturas legales el juez decidirá cuál es la preferente, siendo iguales, se tendrá como tal la primera en tiempo.

Hecha la declaración de la postura preferente, el Juez preguntará si la mejora alguno de los licitadores. En caso de que dentro de los cinco minutos que sigan a la pregunta alguno la mejore, interrogará de nuevo si algún otro postor mejora la puja; y así sucesivamente con respecto a las pujas que se hagan. En cualquier momento en que pasados cinco minutos de hecha la pregunta correspondiente, no se mejore la última postura o puja, declarará el Tribunal fincado el remate en favor del postor que hubiere hecho aquélla.

Artículo 568.- Dentro de los tres días siguientes al en que se fincó el remate, el juez de oficio revisará el procedimiento de ejecución y dictará auto aprobando o no el remate. Contra esta resolución se da el recurso de apelación en ambos efectos cualquiera que sea la cuantía que represente la postura legal.

Article 567. *Once the bids have been* determined to be acceptable, the judge must read them aloud or must order the Secretary to read them, so that the attending bidders can *increase their bids*. If there are several *written bids*, the Judge must decide which is the preferred one, *or* if they are equal, must take the one made at the earliest time.

Once the declaration of the preferred bid has been made, the Judge must ask if any of the bidders want to *increase their bid*. In the event that within five [5] minutes, in response to the question, a *bidder increases their bid*, *the Judge* must again ask if any other bidder *wishes to increase their bid*; and continue this way while bids are made. At any time in which five [5] minutes has passed from *asking for a higher bid*, and not getting a better bid or bid increase over the last bid, the Judge must declare the sale made in favour of the *final* bidder.

Article 568. Within three days following the completion of the auction, the Judge must review the procedures followed during *the auction*, and must issue a court order approving or *not approving* the auction sale. Anyone who has *bid* the amount of the *auction value* has the remedy of appeal against this decision in both effects **[under Mexican law, the entering of an appeal can have either one or two effects on the legal process being appealed – "*both effects*" means the effect of "*devolutivo*," or appeal to a higher court, which by itself would not suspend the legal process under appeal, as well as the effect of "*suspensivo*," the suspension of the legal decision and the process until the appeal is decided].**

Artículo 569.- Una vez que cause estado el auto que aprobó el remate, mandará el juez a solicitud del interesado que dentro de los tres días siguientes se otorgue al comprador la escritura de adjudicación correspondiente, conforme a los términos de su postura, y que se le entreguen los bienes rematados. Asimismo prevendrá al comprador que consigne ante él o ante el Notario que va a autorizar la escritura respectiva el precio del remate.

Si el comprador no consigna el precio en el plazo que el juez le señale, o por su culpa dejaré de tener efecto la venta, se procederá a nueva subasta como si la anterior no se hubiere celebrado, y perderá el postor el depósito a que se refiere el artículo 560 en beneficio del ejecutado, pero se aplicará al ejecutante, si éste lo solicita en abono de su crédito.

Artículo 570.- No habiendo postor, quedará al arbitrio del ejecutante pedir, en el acto de la diligencia o dentro de los tres días que sigan a su celebración, que se le adjudiquen los bienes en el precio que sirvió de base para el remate o que se saquen de nuevo a pública subasta con rebaja del diez por ciento de la tasación.

La segunda y ulteriores subastas se anunciarán mandando publicar un solo edicto y se celebrarán en igual forma que la anterior.

Article 569. Once the court order that approved the auction sale is final, the judge must order, at the request of the petitioner of the lawsuit, that within the next three days the buyer be granted a public document corresponding to the judgement, in accordance with the terms of their bid, and the delivery of the auctioned off goods *to the buyer*. Also *the Judge* must warn the buyer that they must pay before him, or before the *notario* **[civil law notary]** that is going to prepare the corresponding title document, the price of the auction sale.

If the buyer does not pay this amount in the period that the judge has indicated, or, by *the buyer's* fault, *cancels* the sale, a new auction must be held as if the previous *auction* had not taken place, and the bidder will lose the *bid bond* referred to in Article 560 to the benefit of the debtor, but it can be applied to the petitioner of the lawsuit, if they request this in payment of their claim.

Article 570. If there are no bidders, it is left to the discretion of the petitioner of the lawsuit to ask that, on the execution of the Judge's order, or within the next three days after *the auction*, the goods are sold to the petitioner at the price that served as the base for the auction sale **[the auction value]**, or that there is a new public auction with a discount of ten percent from the appraisal.

The second and following auctions must be announced by publishing a single proclamation, and they must be held in the same way in which the previous *auction was held*.

Artículo 571.- Si en las subsecuentes subastas, tampoco hubiere licitadores, el actor podrá pedir o la adjudicación por el precio de la postura legal en la almoneda o que se le entreguen en administración los bienes para aplicar su producto al pago de los intereses y extinción del capital y de las costas.

Artículo 572.- Cualquier liquidación que tenga que hacerse de los gravámenes que afecten a los inmuebles vendidos, gastos de ejecución y demás, se regulará por el juez con un escrito de cada parte y resolución dentro del tercer día la que no admite recurso.

Artículo 573.- Se deroga.

Artículo 574.- Una vez consignado el precio se hará saber al deudor que dentro del tercer día otorgue la escritura de venta a favor del comprador, apercibiéndolo que de no hacerlo, el Juez lo hará en su rebeldía y haciéndolo constar así.

Artículo 575.- Otorgada la escritura se darán al comprador los títulos de propiedad, apremiando en su caso al deudor para que los entregue, y se pondrán los bienes a disposición del mismo comprador, dándose las órdenes necesarias, aún la de desocupación de fincas habitadas por el deudor o por terceros que no tuvieren contrato para acreditar el uso de los bienes con arreglo al Código Civil. También se le dará a conocer como dueño a las personas que para el efecto designe.

Article 571. If in subsequent auctions, there are no bidders, the petitioner of the lawsuit can ask for, or be awarded, the price of the ***auction value*** for the auction, or that the property is delivered to their administration to apply the income **[generated by the property]** to the payment of the interest, extinction of the capital, and the legal costs.

Article 572. Any final payment ***where there are*** liens that affect the sold property, ***legal costs*** and others, must be held by the Judge with a writ to each party and a decision within three days. This decision cannot be appealed.

Article 573. Repealed.

Article 574. Once the price is assigned, it must be made known to the debtor that within three days they must furnish a bill of sale in favour of the buyer, and they must be warned that if they do not do this, because of ***the debtor's*** unwillingness, the Judge must make a ***bill of sale***, and record it that way **[as sold]**.

Article 575. Once the public document is granted, this gives the buyer the title to the property, compelling the debtor to deliver it to ***the buyer***, and put the goods at the disposal of this buyer, giving the necessary orders for the evacuation of property occupied by the debtor or by third parties that do not have a contract to permit their use of the goods in accordance with the Civil Code **[such as a lease or similar arrangement to use the property]**. Also ***the buyer*** must be made known as the owner of the property to those persons ***who have such a contract*** **[such as legal tenants – the property owner's rights in such a contract would transfer to the buyer]**.

Artículo 576.- Con el precio se pagará al acreedor hasta donde alcance y si hubiere costas pendientes de liquidar, se mantendrá en depósito la cantidad que se estime bastante para cubrirlas, hasta que sean aprobadas las que faltaren de pagarse; pero si el ejecutante no formula su liquidación dentro de lo ocho días siguientes al en que se hizo el depósito, a solicitud del ejecutado, podrá el Juez ordenar la devolución.

[El resto de Artículo 576, y Artículos 577 a través de 580 se han omitido porque conciernen a las hipotecas, y no se aplican a la venta de derechos del condominio]

Artículo 581.- Cuando conforme a lo prevenido en el artículo 571, el acreedor hubiere optado por la administración de las fincas embargadas, se observarán las siguientes reglas:

I. El Juez mandará que se haga entrega de ellas bajo el correspondiente inventario y que se le dé a conocer a las personas que el mismo acreedor designe;

II. El acreedor y el deudor podrán establecer, por acuerdos particulares, las condiciones y términos de la administración, forma y época de rendir las cuentas. Si así no lo hicieren, se entenderá que las fincas han de ser administradas según la costumbre del lugar, debiendo el acreedor rendir cuentas cada seis meses;

Article 576. The ***auction price*** must be paid to the creditor ***up to the point where*** it is sufficient ***to cover the debt***, and if there are ***still*** unresolved costs to settle, the amount of an estimate sufficient to cover them must be kept on deposit, until those ***costs or expenses*** that have not been paid are approved; but if the petitioner of the lawsuit does not draw up their ***determination of the amount of these unresolved costs*** within eight **[8]** days following ***the date*** on which the deposit was made, at the request of the debtor, the Judge can order the return ***of the deposit***.

[The remainder of Article 576, as well as Articles 577 through 580 have been omitted because they concern mortgages, and do not apply to the sale of condo rights]

Article 581. When in accordance with the provisions of Article 571, the creditor has chosen to administer the embargoed property, the following rules apply:

I. The Judge must order that delivery of this property be made under the corresponding inventory, and that he be informed of the people that the creditor has designated ***to administer the property***;

II. The creditor and the debtor must establish, by specific agreement, the terms and conditions of the administration ***of the property***, and the manner and times for rendering the accounts. If they do not do this, it is understood that the property must be administered according to the customary practices of its location, with the creditor having to render accounts every six months;

III. Si las fincas fueren rústicas, podrá el deudor intervenir las operaciones de la recolección;

IV. La rendición de cuentas y las diferencias que con motivo de ella surgieren, se substanciarán como se previene para los incidentes;

V. Cuando el ejecutante se haya pagado su crédito, intereses y costas con los productos de las fincas, volverán éstas a poder del ejecutado; y

VI. El acreedor podrá cesar en la administración de la finca, cuando lo crea conveniente, y pedir que continúen los procedimientos de remate con sujeción a este Código, sirviendo de postura legal la misma de la última almoneda celebrada.

[El artículo 582 se ha omitido porque conciernen a las hipotecas, y no se aplican a la venta de derechos del condominio]

Artículo 583.- En el remate de bienes muebles se observarán las disposiciones siguientes:

I. Se anunciará su venta por medio de edictos que se publicarán fijándose diariamente, y durante tres días consecutivos, en la puerta del juzgado y en los tableros y sitios de costumbre, a menos que cualquiera de las partes pida que a su costa se haga también la publicación por algún otro medio;

III. If the property is rural, the debtor can control the operations of the harvest;

IV. The rendering of accounts, and the differences that ***occur*** by reason of unexpected events, must be verified so as to take precautionary actions against these incidents **[from happening again]**;

V. When the petitioner of the lawsuit has been paid the money owed, interest, and legal costs from the income of the property, ***the property*** must return to the control of the debtor;

VI. The creditor can stop administering the property when they believe this is convenient, and ask to continue the procedures of the auction sale in accordance with this Code, with the ***auction value*** being the same one used in the last auction that was held.

[Article 582 has been omitted because it concerns mortgages, and does not apply to the sale of condo rights]

Article 583. In an auction sale of personal property **[as opposed to real estate, which is covered by Article 556]** the following provisions must be observed:

I. The sale must be announced by means of proclamations published daily over three consecutive days, on the door of the courthouse and on bulletin boards and customary places, unless any of the parties ask to also publish them by some other means, at their expense;

II. Si lo pidieren las partes, podrá dispensarse la publicación y mandar hacerse la venta por medio de comisionista o de casa de comercio que expenda objetos o mercancías similares, debiendo hacerse la realización a los precios corrientes en plaza. Si no se consigue dentro de diez días, el Juzgado autorizará una rebaja de diez por ciento de los precios fijados y así sucesivamente, cada diez días, hasta lograr la venta. De ésta se deducirán preferentemente los gastos de comisión que serán de cuenta del deudor;

III. Se cuidará que los bienes estén a la vista y si fueren caldos, semillas u objetos semejantes, que se tenga en el juzgado, a disposición de los licitantes, una muestra. En todo caso estarán a la vista los avalúos;

IV. Si en la almoneda no hubiere postores, se adjudicarán al actor, por el importe de la postura legal, los bienes que elija y basten a cubrir su crédito y las costas; si los bienes fueren de tal naturaleza, que la adjudicación no pueda hacerse sino de todos, también podrá pedirla el acreedor, pero deberá exhibir y entregar de contado el resto del precio, cubierto su crédito y las costas;

V. Si el actor no pidiere la adjudicación, se continuarán sacando a remate los bienes con la retasa del diez por ciento, anunciándose la venta, cada vez, por medio de un solo edicto;

II. At the parties' request, the publication can be dispensed with, and **an order issued** to make the sale by means of a commission agent or a business concern that sells similar items or goods, who must liquidate them at the current market value; if **the liquidation** is not completed within ten days, the Court must authorize a discount of ten percent of the fixed prices, and continue to do so, every ten days, until **the liquidation** is complete. From **the proceeds of the liquidation**, **the liquidators** must deduct preferentially their commission expenses, **and** these must be chargeable to the debtor;

III. The goods must be plainly visible, and if they are broths, seeds, or similar items, there must be in the courthouse, available to the bidders, a sample. In any case, the appraised values must be plainly visible;

IV. If there were no bidders in the auction, the **petitioner of the lawsuit** must be awarded, **up to** the total sum of the **auction value**, the goods that they choose which are sufficient to cover the **money owed to them** and the legal costs; if the goods are of such a nature that they must be awarded as a totality, the creditor can also ask for them, but must immediately pay in cash the price remaining **after** covering the **money owed** and the legal costs;

V. If the **petitioner of the lawsuit** does not ask to be awarded **the goods**, the goods must continue to be put up for auction with a discount of ten percent, advertising the sale, each time, by means of a single proclamation;

VI. Efectuada la venta, se entregarán los bienes al adquiriente, luego que exhiba el precio y se le extenderá la factura correspondiente, que firmará el ejecutado o el Juez en su rebeldía. Lo mismo se observará en el caso de la fracción IV de este artículo; y

VII. En todo lo demás se observarán, en lo conducente, las disposiciones de este Capítulo.

VI. Once the sale has been made, the goods must be surrendered to the buyer, after the price is paid and the corresponding *factura* **[official receipt for tax purposes]** is issued, ***the receipt*** must be signed by the debtor, or by the Judge ***if the debtor is*** unwilling. The same must be observed in the case of subparagraph IV of this article; and

VII. In everything else that is relevant **[to the auction of personal property]**, the provisions of this Chapter apply.

PART 14 – Preventative Injunctions for Lawsuits

Jalisco Code of Civil Procedures
Title Five
Articles 249 – 255

Relevance to a Condominium

When an owner has become significantly delinquent in their fees, or has caused significant problems in the condo, the condo administration can go before a judge and apply to have the private unit sold at public auction under the terms of **Civil Code Article 1032** (see *Part 3 – The Jalisco Condo Law*).

In the documents filed to support the lawsuit, the condo can ask for a "*Medida Precautoria*" (Preventative Measure). If accepted, the Judge will decree an injunction that will direct the local property registry to freeze activity on the property. This prevents the delinquent owner from borrowing against the unit, or transferring its title in any way during the process of the lawsuit. It also prevents third parties from attaching liens.

For more information on how these injunctions are dealt with by the public registry office, see *Part 7 – The Public Registry of Property*.

For more information on how these public property auctions are carried out, see *Part 13 – Rules for Public Property Auctions*.

For practical steps on initiating such a lawsuit, and the steps and time frames involved in the legal process, see our companion book, the "*Jalisco Condo Manual – Second Edition*."

Versions of Laws Used

Codes and laws are living documents that are amended frequently by the level of government that issued them.

This section contains excerpts from the *Código de Procedimientos Civiles del Estado de Jalisco* (Code of Civil Procedures for the State of Jalisco), that took effect on **January 1, 1939**, and was last amended on ***November 29, 2014***.

Sections of the Laws Used

The excerpt from the **Jalisco Code of Civil Procedures** translated in this section is from: *Título Quinto*:

Título Quinto (Title Five) is titled *"De Los Actos Prejudiciales"* (Interlocutory Acts).

CÓDIGO DE PROCEDIMIENTOS CIVILES DEL ESTADO DE JALISCO	JALISCO CODE OF CIVIL PROCEDURES

CÓDIGO DE PROCEDIMIENTOS CIVILES DEL ESTADO DE JALISCO

TÍTULO QUINTO – DE LOS ACTOS PREJUDICIALES

CAPÍTULO VI – De las Providencias Precautorias

SECCIÓN PRIMERA – Disposiciones Generales

Artículo 249.- Antes de iniciarse el juicio, o durante su desarrollo, a solicitud del interesado pueden decretarse todas las medidas necesarias para mantener la situación de hecho o de derecho existentes, así como para garantizar las resultas de una sentencia ejecutoria.

Para decretar cualesquiera de las medidas cautelares a que se refiere este título, el promovente deberá justificar el derecho que le asiste para ello, con prueba documental, y a falta de ésta, con la declaración bajo protesta de dos personas dignas de fe.

Estas providencias se decretarán sin audiencia de la contraparte. Si se solicita después de iniciado el procedimiento se substanciará en expediente por separado ante el mismo juez que conozca del negocio, el cual se identificará con el mismo número del principal, al que se agregará una vez que sea ejecutada la medida.

El Gobierno del estado de Jalisco, a través de sus poderes y los ayuntamientos, estarán exentos de otorgar todas aquellas garantías que en este código se exige a las partes.

JALISCO CODE OF CIVIL PROCEDURES

TITLE FIVE – INTERLOCUTORY ACTS [a decree or judgement issued between the start and end of a legal proceeding]

CHAPTER VI – Preventative Injunctions

FIRST SECTION – General Provisions

Article 249.- Before a trial starts, or during its progress, at the request of the petitioner, all necessary measures to maintain the current circumstances or existing rights can be decreed, as well as to guarantee the results of an executive judgement.

To impose the preventative injunctions to which this title refers on anyone, the claimant must justify the right that supports ***their claim***, with documentary evidence, and, if this is lacking, with a sworn declaration from two trustworthy people.

These injunctions must be decreed in the absence of the other party. If ***the injunctions*** are requested after the start of the ***legal*** proceeding, ***the claimant*** must provide separate written evidence before the same Judge who ***is carrying out the trial***, who must identify ***the claim*** with the same number as the main trial, to which it must be added once the injunction is executed ***by the Judge***.

The Government of the State of Jalisco, through its ***agencies*** and the municipal councils, are exempt from granting all those guarantees that are demanded of the parties in this Code **[if you're suing the State Government, none of this applies]**.

En los asuntos de familia, el Juez de la causa podrá decretar las órdenes de protección previstas por la Ley General de Acceso a las Mujeres a una Vida Libre de Violencia.

Artículo 250.- Será competente para decretar las providencias cautelares el juez que lo sea para conocer de la demanda principal. En caso de urgencia también podrá decretarlas el del lugar en que deban efectuarse. En este último caso, una vez ejecutada o resuelta la reclamación, se remitirán las actuaciones al órgano competente.

Artículo 251.- De toda providencia precautoria queda responsable el que la pida, y si no se funda en instrumento público o título ejecutivo, el solicitante otorgará garantía bastante en cualesquiera de las formas previstas por la ley cuyo monto será fijado discrecionalmente por el juez, para asegurar el pago de los daños y perjuicios que se ocasionen, ya porque se revoque la providencia o ya porque entablada la demanda, sea absuelto el demandado. Mientras no se exhiba la garantía no podrá decretarse la medida.

Artículo 252.- La resolución que conceda la medida solicitada, así como su ejecución no admite recurso alguno, ni aquella prejuzga sobre la legalidad de la situación que se mantiene, ni sobre los derechos o responsabilidades del que la solicitó; la que la niegue será apelable. La tramitación y las resoluciones de estas medidas serán de carácter reservado.

Efectuada la providencia precautoria antes de ser entablada la demanda, el que la pidió deberá interponerla dentro de los diez días siguientes.

In family matters, the Trial Judge can decree the orders of protection provided by the General Law of Access to Women to a Violence-Free Life.

Article 250.- The judge who ***is conducting*** the main lawsuit has the authority to decree preventative injunctions. In a case of urgent need, he can also decree ***preventative injunctions*** for the place in which they should take effect. In this latter case, once ***the injunctions*** have been executed, or the complaint has been resolved, the judicial actions return to the competent authority.

Article 251.- For every claimed preventative injunction that remains answerable, and if it is not based on a public document or a writ of execution, the petitioner must pay a sufficient guarantee in any of the forms provided by law, whose amount will be fixed at the discretion of the Judge, to assure the payment of the damages and losses caused, because the injunction is revoked, or, once the lawsuit has started, the defendant is acquitted. As long as this guarantee has not been paid, the injunction cannot be decreed.

Article 252.- The decision that grants the requested injunction, as well as its enforcement, cannot be appealed, nor does it prejudice the legality of the continuing legal proceeding, nor the rights or responsibilities of the petitioner; ***an injunction*** that is denied can be appealed. The application process and the decision process for these injunctions must be of a private nature **[between the judge and the petitioner]**.

To bring about a preventative injunction before the lawsuit is decreed, the petitioner must file it within the next ten **[10]** days.

Artículo 253.- El ejecutado podrá reclamar la providencia en cualquier tiempo hasta antes de la sentencia ejecutoria; para cuyo efecto se le notificará la ejecución de aquella, en caso de no haberse practicado la diligencia con su persona o la de su representante legítimo. La reclamación deberá fundarse en que no se practicó de acuerdo con la ley.
También lo puede hacer un tercero cuando sus bienes hayan sido objeto de la medida ejecutada.

En ambos casos deberán de substanciarse en forma incidental. La resolución que se dicte será apelable sólo en el efecto devolutivo.

Artículo 254.- No se llevará a cabo la providencia precautoria, o se levantará de plano y bajo responsabilidad del juez, la que hubiere practicado, si el perjudicado:

I. Consigna el valor u objeto pretendido;

II. Da caución para responder de lo reclamado, salvo en el caso de que se trate de preservar un derecho que de no hacerlo entrañe una vejación o descrédito o bien un perjuicio de orden moral;

III. Lo solicita transcurrido el plazo fijado por el juez sin que se hubiere presentado la demanda, cuando fuese decretada como acto prejudicial;

Article 253.- The debtor whose property is attached can file a claim against the injunction at any time, even before the executive judgement; for which effect they must be notified of the execution of ***the injunction***, in the event that due diligence was not practiced towards the person or their legal representative. The complaint must be based on ***the injunction*** not being carried out according to law. A third party can also file a complaint against ***the injunction*** when their goods have been subjected to the executed measure.

In both cases, they must provide evidence in a related form. The decision ***of the Judge*** can only be appealed with the devolutive effect **[under Mexican law, the entering of an appeal with "*efecto devolutivo*" is an appeal to a higher court which does not suspend or interrupt the legal process under appeal]**.

Article 254.- The preventative injunction cannot take effect, or ***come*** under the responsibility of the Judge that would have ***enforced*** it, if the petitioner:

I. ***Writes about*** a fake value or object ***in their application***;

II. Uses caution **[reluctant to answer or provide details]** when questioned about what is claimed, except in the case of trying to preserve a right that by not taking it will cause aggravation, discredit, or damage of a moral kind **[non-material damages]**;

III. Requests it after the period fixed by the Judge has passed without presenting the lawsuit document, when it was decreed as an interlocutory act **[a decree or judgement issued in an intermediate stage between the start and end of a legal proceeding]**;

IV. Obtiene resolución favorable en su reclamación;

V. Prueba tener bienes raíces suficientes para responder del éxito de la demanda;

VI. Es un tercero y acredita por manifestación auténtica del Registro Público de la Propiedad que los bienes que se reclaman están inscritos a su nombre; y

VII. Obtiene sentencia definitiva favorable.

Contra la resolución que se dicte en estos casos no procede recurso.

Artículo 255.- Podrá solicitarse y decretarse la incorporación al Registro Público de la Propiedad, de las resoluciones judiciales en que se admita una demanda cuyos efectos, en caso de prosperar, alteren la situación de bienes o derechos cuya inscripción sea indispensable en la citada oficina, la que no se decretará si no se otorga previamente garantía que prudentemente fijará el juez, para responder de los daños que resulten por la inscripción.

IV. Obtains a favourable decision in their claim;

V. Tries to possess real estate sufficient to account for the success of the lawsuit;

VI. They are a third party, and verified by a legal declaration from the Public Registry Of Property that the goods being claimed are on record as being in their name; and

VII. Obtains a favourable final judgment.

There is no appeal gainst the decision that is made in these cases.

Article 255. The incorporation into the Public Registry of Property can be requested and decreed for the judge's decisions in which a lawsuit is recognised whose effects, in case of being successful, modify the state of goods or rights whose registration exists in the *Public Registry*. This cannot be decreed *by the Judge* if a guarantee that was set by the judge, after due consideration, has not been previously paid to respond to the damages that result from the registration.

PART 15 – Example of Sanctions

Condominium Real Estate Property Law for the Federal District
Title 8
Articles 86 – 89

Relevance to Condominiums in Jalisco

Many states in México have modelled their condo legislation on that of the D.F. (Federal District).

Jalisco decided to take a different approach, and the Jalisco condo law in the Civil Code differs in some significant ways from that of the D.F. (and other states).

One of these differences is sanctions.

The condo law in the D.F. has a robust set of sanctions that condos can apply both against problem owners, and the administration itself. The Jalisco condo law lacks these.

Since these are a useful tool, even without the force of state law behind them, they can be added to a condo's by-laws.

If you decide to go this route, this excerpt from the condo law of the D.F. will give you a good basis for drafting suitable by-law articles for your condo.

If you do this, always run the final by-law language past a *notario* (civil law notary) to make sure they're properly drafted, and don't contradict any other laws, before you present them for approval at an Extraordinary Assembly.

> **IMPORTANT**: the laws set out in this chapter **do not apply to a condo in the state of Jalisco**. They are presented only as a model to use to create by-law articles with a similar function.

Versions of Laws Used

Codes and laws are living documents that are amended frequently by the level of government that issued them.

This section contains an excerpt from the *Ley de Propiedad en Condominio de Inmuebles para el Distrito Federal* (Condominium Real Estate Property Law for the Federal District), that took effect on **January 7, 1999**, and was last amended on ***November 28, 2014.***

This law was amended after the last edition was published, and has been updated in this edition.

I believe this law was originally part of the Civil Code for the D.F. before being broken out as a separate law.

Sections of the Laws Used

The excerpt from the **Condo Law of the D.F.** translated in this section is *Título Octavo*:

Título Octavo (Title Eight) is titled *"De Las Sanciones"* (Sanctions).

LEY DE PROPIEDAD EN CONDOMINIO DE INMUEBLES PARA EL DISTRITO FEDERAL

TÍTULO OCTAVO – DE LAS SANCIONES

CAPÍTULO ÚNICO

Artículo 86.- Las violaciones a lo establecido por la presente Ley, su Reglamento y demás disposiciones que de ella emanen, serán sancionadas por la Procuraduría en el ámbito de su competencia. Lo anterior será de acuerdo a lo establecido en la presente Ley, su Reglamento, Escritura Constitutiva y Reglamento Interno.

Artículo 87.- La contravención a las disposiciones de esta ley establecidas en los artículos 14, 16, 19, 21, 25, 43, 44, 49, 59 y 73, serán sancionadas con multa que se aplicará de acuerdo con los siguientes criterios:

CONDOMINIUM REAL ESTATE PROPERTY LAW FOR THE FEDERAL DISTRICT

TITLE EIGHT – SANCTIONS

ONLY CHAPTER – Sanctions

Article 86.- The violations of *rules* established by this Law **[the condo law for the D.F.]**, its Regulations, and other provisions arising from it, can be penalised by the Office of the Attorney General within its area of jurisdiction. The foregoing *penalties* must be in accordance with this Law, its Regulations, *the condo's* establishing document, and *the condo's* by-laws.

Article 87.- A breach of the provisions of this law **[the condo law of the D.F.]** that are established in articles 14 **[ownership rights in common property are an integral part of each private unit and cannot be separated or sold]**, 16 **[right to enjoy common property without restricting others – also lists the owner's rights]**, 19 **[who represents a title holder to carry out the owner's obligations]**, 21 **[a list of prohibited actions including breaking the peace, making modifications without permission, and owning pets that annoy others]**, 25 **[restrictions on owners in condo apartments]**, 43 **[duties of the Administrator]**, 44 **[outgoing Administrator must turn over documentation to incoming Administrator]**, 49 **[duties of the Oversight Committee (Council or Board)]**, 59 **[payment of fees and late penalties]** and 73 **[arbitration and ability of the Attorney General's Office to uphold sanctions]** can be punished with a fine that is applied according to the following criteria:

I. Por faltas que afecten la tranquilidad o la comodidad de la vida condominal, se aplicará multa por el equivalente de diez a cien veces la Unidad de Cuenta de la Ciudad de México vigente;

I. For violations that affect the tranquillity or the comfort of condominium life, a fine can be applied that is the equivalent of from ten **[10]** to one-hundred **[100]** times the Accounting Unit of Mexico City now in effect **[a new unit established at the end of 2014 for determining a standard value for fines and penalties – replaces *"días de salario mínimo general vigente en el Distrito Federal"* (days of the general minimum wage in effect in the Federal District)]**;

II. Por faltas que afecten el estado físico del inmueble sin que esto signifique poner en riesgo la seguridad de los demás condóminos; que impidan u obstaculicen el uso adecuado de las instalaciones y áreas comunes; o que afecten el funcionamiento del condominio, se aplicará multa por el equivalente de cincuenta a doscientos veces la Unidad de Cuenta de la Ciudad de México vigente;

II. For violations that affect the physical condition of the *condo property* without a significant risk to the security of the other owners; that impede or obstruct proper use of the facilities and the common areas; or which affect the functioning of the condominium, a fine can be applied that is the equivalent of from fifty **[50]** to two-hundred **[200]** times the Accounting Unit of Mexico City now in effect;

III. Por aquellas faltas que provoquen un daño patrimonial, o pongan en riesgo la seguridad del inmueble o las personas, se aplicará multa por el equivalente de cincuenta a trescientos veces la Unidad de Cuenta de la Ciudad de México vigente;

III. For those violations that bring about property damage, or which put at risk the security of the *condo property* or people, a fine can be applied that is the equivalent of from fifty **[50]** to three-hundred **[300]** times the Accounting Unit of Mexico City now in effect;

IV. Por incumplimiento en el pago oportuno de las cuotas ordinarias, extraordinarias de administración, de mantenimiento y las correspondientes al fondo de reserva, se aplicará multa de 10 a 100 veces la Unidad de Cuenta de la Ciudad de México vigente;

IV. For failure to expediently pay ordinary fees, extraordinary administration *fees* **[assessments]**, *fees* for maintenance, and *fees* pertaining to the reserve fund, a fine can be applied from 10 to 100 times the Accounting Unit of Mexico City now in effect;

V. Los Administradores o Comités de Vigilancia que a juicio de la Asamblea General, Consejo, o de la Procuraduría no hagan un buen manejo o vigilancia de las cuotas de servicios, mantenimiento y administración, de reserva o extraordinarias, por el abuso de su cargo o incumplimiento de sus funciones, o se ostenten como tal sin cumplir lo que esta Ley y su reglamento establecen para su designación, estarán sujetos a las sanciones establecidas en las fracciones I, II, III y IV de este artículo, aumentando un 50% la sanción que le corresponda, independientemente de las responsabilidades o sanciones a que haya lugar, contempladas en otras Leyes;

VI. Se aplicará multa de 50 a 200 veces la Unidad de Cuenta de la Ciudad de México vigente al administrador o persona que tenga bajo su custodia el libro de actas debidamente autorizado y que habiendo sido notificado de una Asamblea General legalmente constituida no lo presente para el desahogo de la misma;

VII. Se aplicará multa de 50 a 300 veces la Unidad de Cuenta de la Ciudad de México vigente por incumplimiento a lo dispuesto en el artículo 44 de la presente Ley. En los casos de reincidencia, se aplicará hasta el doble de la sanción originalmente impuesta; y

V. Administrators or oversight committees **[Councils or Boards]** that, in the judgement of the General Assembly, Council **[Board]**, or the Attorney General's Office, have not handled or monitored the fees for services, maintenance and administration, the reserves or *assessments* properly, by the abuse of their office or failure to fulfil their duties, or to hold such office without obeying *those rules* that this Law and *the condo's* by-laws set out for their appointment, can be subject to the sanctions established in parts I, II, III, and IV of this article, increasing by 50% the corresponding sanction, independently of the accountabilities or sanctions already in place, *or* contemplated in other Laws;

VI. A fine from 50 to 200 times the Accounting Unit of Mexico City now in effect can be applied to the Administrator or person that has custody of the duly authorised minutes book, and, having been notified of a legally constituted General Assembly, does not present *the minute book* for its use *at the assembly*;

VII. A fine from 50 to 300 times the Accounting Unit of Mexico City now in effect can be applied for failure to comply with *the requirements of* Article 44 of this Law **[outgoing Administrator must turn over documentation to incoming Administrator]**. In cases of a recurring *violation*, *a fine* can be applied up to double the sanction originally imposed; and

VIII. Se aplicara multa de 100 a 400 veces la Unidad de Cuenta de la Ciudad de México vigente, a los administradores que realicen cobros no previstos en esta ley y aprobados por la Asamblea General en viviendas de interés social y popular. En los casos de reincidencia, se aplicará hasta el doble de la sanción originalmente impuesta.

Artículo 88.- Las sanciones establecidas en la presente Ley se aplicarán independientemente de las que se impongan por la violación de otras disposiciones aplicables. La Asamblea General podrá resolver en una reunión especial convocada para tal efecto y de acuerdo a lo establecido en el **artículo 32** de la presente Ley, para tomar las siguientes medidas:

I. Iniciar las acciones civiles correspondientes para exigir al condómino que incumpla con las obligaciones establecidas en la presente Ley, o las contenidas en la Escritura Constitutiva o en los acuerdos de la propia Asamblea General o en el Reglamento Interno, el cumplimiento forzoso de dichas obligaciones; y

II. En caso de que dicho incumplimiento sea reiterado o grave, se podrá demandar ante los juzgados civiles, la imposición de las sanciones pecuniarias que se hubieren previsto, las cuales podrán llegar incluso hasta la enajenación del inmueble y la rescisión del contrato que le permite ser poseedor derivado.

VIII. A fine from 100 to 400 times the Accounting Unit of Mexico City now in effect can be applied to the administrators that carry out collections not foreseen in this law and approved by the General Assembly in low-cost public housing. In cases of a recurring *violation*, *a fine* can be applied up to double the sanction originally imposed.

Article 88.- The sanctions established in this Law can be applied independently of those imposed for violations of other applicable rules. The General Assembly **[condo assembly]** can adopt a resolution at a special meeting convened for this purpose **[an extraordinary assembly]**, and, in accordance with that which is established in **Article 32** of this Law **[procedures for holding an assembly]**, the following measures can be taken:

I. Begin appropriate civil actions to demand an owner that does not comply with the obligations established in this Law, or those contained in the establishing public document, or in the agreements of the *condo's* General Assembly, or in *the condo's* by-laws, the forced fulfilment of these aforementioned obligations; and

II. In the event the aforementioned nonfulfilment *of obligations* is repeated or serious, then *the condo* can file a claim in the civil court, *for* the assessment of the financial penalties that are allowed, which can even include the sale of the property and the annulment of a contract that enables *the violator* to be the derivative owner *of the property* **[lawful possession arising from a contract (such as a tenancy agreement), without ownership of the property – this allows eviction of a tenant].**

III. Solicitar a la Delegación ordene la verificación administrativa cuando se estén realizando obras sin las autorizaciones correspondientes en áreas comunes. Facilitando la Asamblea General el acceso al condominio a las autoridades para realizar la visita de verificación y ejecutar las sanciones que de ello deriven.

Artículo 89.- Para la imposición de las sanciones la Procuraduría deberá adoptar las medidas de apremio de acuerdo a lo establecido Ley de la Procuraduría Social del Distrito Federal, así como de la verificación e inspección a fin de emitir sus resoluciones, de conformidad al procedimiento previsto en la Ley de Procedimiento Administrativo del Distrito Federal. En contra de esas resoluciones los afectados podrán, a su elección, interponer el recurso de inconformidad previsto en la Ley antes citada o interponer el juicio de nulidad ante el Tribunal de lo Contencioso Administrativo del Distrito Federal.

III. When work without the proper authorisation **is being done** in the common areas, request that the *Delegación* **[municipal government]** order an administrative investigation. **By which** the General Assembly facilitates access to the condominium to the authorities **for them** to carry out their **investigation** and to **enforce** the resulting sanctions.

Article 89.- For the imposition of sanctions, the Attorney General's Office must adopt the enforcement measures in accordance with the Law of the Civil Attorney General's Office for the Federal District, as well as the verification and inspection needed to issue its decisions, in accordance with the procedures **set out** in the Law of Administrative Procedure of the Federal District. In opposition to these decisions, those affected can, at their option, **have** the recourse to disagree as **set out** in the above-mentioned Law, or to **attempt** a proceeding for annulment before the Court for Administrative Conflicts of the Federal District.

JaliscoCondos.org Web Site

JaliscoCondos.org is committed to giving you the most comprehensive and accurate information about running a condo in the state of Jalisco.

Here's the current site layout:

Home Page: gives you information about our books and online resources. You can opt-in to be notified by email when new books are published, or when new content is added to the web site.

Blog: lets you know about corrections to the books, expands on topics covered by the books, and discusses other topics relevant to condos in Jalisco. User's comments to the articles give the perspective and experience of others. You can subscribe to the blog, to receive an email whenever there's a new blog post.

Here's our implementation plan for future online features:

The online edition of the "*Jalisco Condo Law in English – Second Edition*": *coming late-2015* – will be an online version of the entire text from the book.

You can choose a book section, or an entire code or law, and then display all articles from your chosen section in the same side-by-side format used in the book (synchronised Spanish and English).

You can search the article display in either English or Spanish, and reduce the number of articles displayed to only those that contain your search word or phrase.

This site is also mobile friendly, and will work equally well on smartphones, tablets, laptops, or desktops.

Future Site Additions: we plan to add subscription-based, in-depth video training modules covering each main topic from the "*Jalisco Condo Manual – Second Edition*." Each topic will be broken into sections, with reviews and quizzes to help you assess your online learning. You'll be able to access these at any time to suit your schedule.

Condo Site Hosting: we plan to add hosting and design services for condo web sites. A condo web site is the most efficient and effective communication tool available to a condo administration. You'll be able to have a customised web site, specifically designed to suit the needs of your condo, up and running in a few days. Maintenance and content additions can be done by anyone. All this for a one-time setup fee, plus a modest annual hosting fee.

"An accessible and searchable online version of this book"

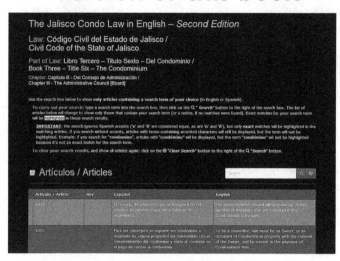

Online Edition of the *"Jalisco Condo Law in English - Second Edition"*

Coming late-2015

In late-2015 we're launching an exciting new development for condo owners and administrators – an online version of the *"Jalisco Condo Law in English – Second Edition."*

It works well as a companion to the printed edition, or as an alternative to it.

Every article of every code or law that appears in the book is available in the online database.

You just select the code or law you want to see. You can narrow this down to a particular section, or a particular chapter, or view the entire law.

You will then be shown all articles that were excerpted and translated in the book that match your selection.

These are presented in a side-by-side format showing the original Spanish text along-side the English translation.

The article view is searchable in English or Spanish (accents are ignored in a search). This will reduce the displayed articles to only those containing the word or phrase you searched for.

In addition, the format is designed specifically for mobile devices. You can use all these features, and view the translations, on a smartphone, tablet, laptop, or desktop – at your convenience.

Access will be by yearly subscription, and additions and updates to the book will be available to you instantly – no need to wait for the next edition of the book!

"ESSENTIAL READING FOR ANYONE LIVING IN OR BUYING A CONDO"

Jalisco Condo Manual - Second Edition

a step-by-step guide and reference manual for condos in Jalisco

- *If you own a condo apartment or a house in a gated condo,* you should be aware of the most common mistakes your condo administration might be making that can affect the value of your property.

- *If you're a member of a condo administration*, you owe it to yourself, and the homeowners you represent, to make sure your condominium is being run properly, efficiently, and in compliance with the state condo law.

- *If you're thinking about buying a condo*, you need to be able to tell whether the condo is being administered properly. This could directly affect both your experience as a resident, and your future property value.

- *If you're a real-estate agent*, you owe it to your clients to be able to spot any problems with the way the condos you show your clients are being run.

You've probably found that there's widespread misinformation circulating about the nuts and bolts of running a condo in the state of Jalisco – assuming you can find any reliable info at all!

Much of the problem comes from unsubstantiated opinions or maintaining the status quo. Some early condos made mistakes when they were set-up, and these have been continued by new condos copying them! Eventually, poor (and often, illegal) practices became the standards on which new condo administrations are based. The real problem is that detailed and accurate information has not been available to you.

Until now . . .

This book grew out of the author's own frustration with this same problem. After doing several years of research, he gathered together all the information needed for you to properly administer a condo according to the Jalisco condo law, and organised it for you into a single book. At first, you can use it as a learning guide, and then as a day-to-day reference.

What you'll learn from this book:

- The two different types of condo meetings and their purpose
- How to correctly carry out votes and elections
- How to accept legal proxies
- The correct way to collect fees
- How to collect from overdue owners, including the process of forcing the sale of a unit at public auction
- The rights and duties of owners, the Administrator, and the Council (Board)
- How to overcome owner dissatisfaction by using effective communications
- How to conduct board and committee meetings
- How to maintain condo records
- How to conform with the new tax laws of 2014
- The differences made by the year your condo was set up
- And much more ...

As well as in-depth information, you also get many sample forms and other documents – all useful in the day to day running of a condo.

For more information visit **www.jaliscocondos.org**

Coming Soon **Upcoming Books from JaliscoCondos.org**

How to Prepare & Track a Condo Budget - a step-by-step tutorial

An accurate budget is vital to the year-to-year management of your condominium.

Preparing a budget that covers all regular expenses, that gives you an adequate contingency for unknown expenses, and sets out planned reserve contributions and expenditures, is the mark of a competent condo administration.

This tutorial guides you step-by-step through the preparation of a sound budget, as well as showing you how to track the actual expenses vs. the budget throughout the year.

This tracking process forms the basis for the Administrator's monthly reports to the Council, and the legally-required quarterly reports to the community. As well, it gives you experience-based data for preparing the following year's budget.

How to Carry Out Your Own Condo Reserve Study

Condo reserve funds aren't only a legal requirement, they're also the corner-stone of proper financial management.

Dart-board approaches based on a percentage of condo fees or some arbitrary number of months of expenses just don't work.

Proper reserve fund management is based on the planned funding and scheduling of repairs and maintenance of the condo assets over their life. A reserve study both anticipates these expenses, and plans for them to occur.

The end result is proper maintenance of the common property (resulting in higher property values), along with the ability to pay for major replacements and refurbishments without the need for special assessments.

This book shows you step-by-step how to carry out and update your own condo reserve study, and come up with a reserve funding plan and maintenance schedule for your condo assets.

How To Write Effective Condo By-Laws

While the state condo legislation gives the framework and structure for the condominium and its management, these should be supplemented with additional by-laws that suit the specific needs of your condo.

Condo by-laws often suffer from common problems such as:

contradicting the condo law, or being unenforceable;

being vague, and open to interpretation;

contradicting themselves;

overlooking important regulations; or

being overzealous and controlling.

This book will give you in-depth information, plus effective tips based on experience. Together, these will allow you to come up with a set of reasonable, enforceable by-laws that'll significantly aid your condo administration, as well as give you a practical set of rules for the community.

Translation Practices

To make the English translations flow more naturally, I might have changed the punctuation, or rearranged the order of the words.

For added clarity, I might have included extra or implied words or phrases in the English translation that don't appear in the original Spanish text. Sometimes a confusing phrase in Spanish has been clarified in English with something that is not a direct or obvious translation. In both cases, these are shown by ***bolded italic text*** in the translation. These are intended to make the text clearer (particularly vague Spanish pronoun references, that can cause confusion), and should not change the meaning.

> For example, if a long article started off with "*In a compound condominium... ,*" went on to describe various attributes of a compound condo, and ended in "*...and those living in **it**,*" I would translate this last part as, "*...and those living in **the compound condominium***" to make the reference for the pronoun "***it***" clear.

In-line notes have also been added in **[bolded text between square brackets]**. These editorial notes aren't part of the translation, and don't appear in the original Spanish text. They are there to clarify the text or explain legal concepts.

Spanish Terms in the English Text

Sometimes it's necessary to use a spanish term in the translated text. When I first introduce a Spanish concept, term, or name, I'll show it in Spanish *highlighted in italics*, followed by the English translation in parentheses.

Later uses of the term will also be *highlighted in italics*, but might no longer be followed by the English translation.

Gender-Neutral Pronouns in the English Text

I've eliminated all gender-specific pronouns such as "*he,*" "*his,*" or "*her,*" that do not refer to specific objects, by replacing them with the singular "*they*" form ("*they,*" "*their,*" "*them*, and "*themself*"). This issue is unique to English, and doesn't exist in the original Spanish.

This is much preferable to clumsy and distracting constructs such as "*he or she,*" "*he/she,*" or "*s/he.*" In addition, these don't work to repace "*his*" or "*her*".

> For example, rather than, "*...the Administrator or **his/her** assistant...*" I've would use, "*...the Administrator or **their** assistant...*".

English Language and Spellings Used in this Book

This book is written in **International English** – rather than American English.

International English uses spellings adopted by nearly all English-speaking nations in the world **with the exception of the U.S., and its various territories**.

These spellings, in many cases, differ from spellings used in the U.S.

For example:

labour rather than **labor**,

centre rather than **center**, or

authorise rather than **authorize**.

My reasons for adopting this version of English for my book are as follows:

1. our company isn't located in the U.S.;
2. this book deals with issues specifically about living in México (a non-English country); and
3. this book is intended for an international English-speaking audience from such diverse regions as: Canada, the U.S., México, the U.K., Ireland, Australia, and the European Union.

Index

A

W

CPSIA information can be obtained
at www.ICGtesting.com
Printed in the USA
BVHW060148300120
570846BV00009B/320